GOLDEN AGE GODDESSES

Love, Abundance and Truth Have Returned

By LALITHA DONATELLA RIBACK

SOULFUL VALLEY PUBLISHING

Copyright © 2025 by Lalitha Donatella Riback
Published by Katie Carey of Soulful Valley Publishing

All rights reserved. Apart from any fair dealing for the purposes of research, private study, criticism, or review, as permitted under the Copyright, Designs and Patents Act of 1988, this publication may only be reproduced, stored, or transmitted in any form or by any means with the prior permission in writing of the copyright owner, or in this case, of the reprographic reproduction in accordance with the terms of licensees issued by the Copyright Licensing Agency. Enquiries concerning reproduction outside those terms should be sent to the publisher.

Disclaimer

The publisher and the author provide this book on an "as is" basis and make no representations or warranties of any kind concerning the book or its contents. They disclaim all such representations and warranties of healthcare for a particular purpose. In addition, the publisher and the author assume no responsibility for errors, inaccuracies, omissions, or any other consistency herein.

The content of this book is for informational purposes only and is not intended to diagnose, treat, cure, or prevent any condition or disease. You understand this book is not intended as a substitute for consultation with a licensed practitioner. Please consult with your own physician or healthcare specialist regarding the suggestions and recommendations made in this book. The use of this book implies your acceptance of this disclaimer.

The publisher and the author make no guarantees concerning the level of success you may experience by following the advice and strategies contained in this book, and you accept the risk that results will differ for each individual. The testimonials and examples provided in this book show exceptional results which may not apply to the average reader and are not intended to represent or guarantee that you will achieve the same or similar results.

This is a work of creative nonfiction. The events portrayed have been done so to the best of each author's memory. While all the stories in this book are true, some names and identifying details may have been changed to protect the privacy of the people involved.

Table of Contents

ACKNOWLEDGEMENTS 6
INTRODUCTION 8
    EVENTS THAT STARTED THIS BOOK 8
CHAPTER 1 13
    LALITA TRIPURA SUNDARI 13
CHAPTER 2 35
    THE DIVINE FEMININE IS LOVE 35
CHAPTER 3 49
    GODDESS BONA DEA AND HER SECRET POWERS 49
CHAPTER 4 65
    VESTA, THE GODDESS OF FIRE AND THE HEARTH 65
CHAPTER 5 127
    DURGA MATA 127
CHAPTER 6 133
    MEENAKSHI, THE SUPREME GODDESS OF MADURAI
    133
CHAPTER 7 150
    THE MYSTERY OF MARY MAGDALENE 150
CHAPTER 8 177
    GODDESS RUACH 177
CHAPTER 9 186

RAKAKSHI AND THE WISH-FULFILLING GEM............ 186
EPILOGUE 193
   HOW TO CONNECT WITH THE GODDESS 193
BIOGRAPHY 198
BIBLIOGRAPHY 200

ACKNOWLEDGEMENTS

My infinite gratitude goes to my teacher Dr. Pillai and the Goddesses for their grace and inspiration. I also dedicate this book with love to my family: Frank, Randy and Becky, Nick and Shannon.

INTRODUCTION

EVENTS THAT STARTED THIS BOOK

The Goddess is the epitome of love. She will rule the Golden Age. -Dr. Pillai

I didn't want to write another book. In fact, when my latest book "Think and Receive Miracles" was published in May 2024, I just wanted a vacation. But everything changed a few days later when the idea of the Goddess archetype installed itself in my mind, and didn't leave me.

After decades on the spiritual path, I've learned to recognize divine synchronicity, and if your Source wants you to reach a particular goal, your ego may put up a fight, but the Divine will invariably win.

This time, too, I noticed an avalanche of hints from articles on the Goddess, Goddess chants, and my memories of a 10-day India trip visiting Goddess temples. I also remembered traveling to hundreds of other power vortexes connected with Goddesses. Yet refusing to engage in more writing, I thought:

I will not do this.

But a few days later I woke up around 4 a.m. and heard my own voice speaking to the Mother Goddess, calling her: "Ma, Ma, Ma." Multiple times I repeated "Ma," a word that means Divine Mother in Tamil—a language that I don't speak, even though I've learned many Tamil mantras in mystery school studies with my teacher, Dr. Pillai.

Tears and deep emotions indicated that an important soul event had just occurred in the dream state. But no matter how much I tried; I could not remember it.

Again, later that day, I came across several books with Goddess titles, images of Goddesses from the Hindu, Buddhist and Japanese traditions, and more Goddess videos. Then most staggering, an audio file started playing on iTunes by itself: it was a Goddess mantra that I had forgotten.

And finally, a Sanskrit chant praising a form of the Goddess came to me fortuitously on social media. I got blissfully lost in its divine lyrics, and my ego softened. I was almost ready to surrender.

It was obvious that the Goddesses of the universe did not want me to forget them, and the nagging feeling that I must embark on a new book adventure remained. However, making one last attempt to refuse, I asked for guidance, speaking directly to my Higher Self, the God Self that is within us:

Should I really write a book about the Divine Feminine?

I hoped for a negative response, but immediately, like a flash of light, a dazzling memory surfaced—my mystical and profound encounter with a Goddess 11 years ago at a spiritual retreat in India.

Soon after came more memories of life-altering visions of Goddesses during another India trip. Both these images and their cosmic meanings filled my mind with such great longing and gratitude that I finally let go of my resistance. I relaxed:

Message received—I will write the book. Thank you.

After these thoughts and within just a few minutes, I began thinking about the introduction to this book. More memories of my lifelong experiences with the Goddess began coming like unstoppable sea waves. My negativity, sorrow, worries and concerns vanished, and with nothing else in the way I began writing.

So here you are. And I hope you'll be inspired to embody the divine feminine powers of love, compassion, the ability to create galaxies, and reach higher states of awareness and union with the divine—abilities traditionally connected with the Goddess archetype.

I know this might sound like hype, but the yogis of India, especially the Tamil Siddhas—the most ancient tradition of adepts with supernormal powers—consider creating a galaxy a doable feat for an enlightened human.

If you have a scientific mind, your interest might lean more towards technology. And you will find in this book some references to new science that validates the existence of a loftier cosmology. However, I believe that spiritual technology and spiritual growth are necessary for the evolution of the human species, or we might turn into lifeless machines.

What Can You Expect from Connecting with the Goddesses?

From my mystery school studies of several Goddess traditions, life experiences and ongoing intuitive insights, I know that the Goddesses can:

- Help you experience Heaven while you are still here on Earth, bringing you more love, abundance, and wisdom. Everything belongs to the Mother Goddess.
- Stretch the limits of your personality and conception of the cosmos.
- Help you decode notions of physics, astronomy and mathematics without studying them. This is something that

happened to a man named Srinivasa Iyengar Ramanujan, a Cambridge genius mathematician who received all his knowledge from Goddess Lakshmi.

- Reveal to you symbols and truths of the universe.
- Expand the boundaries of your consciousness to reach the highest spiritual peaks and take you high up above the highest heavens.
- Raise your frequency, self-esteem, bring you bliss, and transform you into a human angel of light.

And through their various roles and divine qualities, the Goddesses will contribute to the flourishing of a Golden Age on Earth, where higher knowledge, everlasting prosperity, total protection from evil, and true love will abound.

This new divine cycle that started a year ago, in December 2023, will facilitate your ascension to a higher dimension and lead to your spiritual evolution.

As you learn about these Goddesses, their attributes of infinite joy, supernormal powers and deep love for all life can become yours. The Goddesses are ready to bless you with wish fulfillment, loving relationships, pure beauty, and incredible abundance. May the beginning of Satya Yuga or the Golden Age restore all your lost divine DNA and supernormal powers.

CHAPTER 1

LALITA TRIPURA SUNDARI

On her feet She wears anklets,
She dons a red silk dress…
She carries flower arrows…
On her lovely head she wears the diadem,
On her ears She wears earrings
Of bluish radiant gems.
-Siddhar Thirumoolar – "Tripurai's Form"

She appeared unexpectedly. Her smiling sideway glance, incredible beauty, and regal authority completely filled my vision with her breathtaking presence. I recognized her as Lalita Tripura Sundari, the Divine Mother.

I intuitively knew that the dark space or cosmic void behind her contained total potentiality—a paradox of coexisting emptiness and fullness. But these terms actually came from my recent research because, at that time, all I saw was the Goddess in a dark, empty space full of energy, beauty and divinity.

Her long black hair, styled back behind her small ears, revealed her delicate white face illuminated by a gold-red glow.

The large eyes exuded motherly love and regal confidence, and I marveled at her vermillion dress, adorned with shimmering emerald fabric and a wide golden hem. Her face shined with unmatched beauty, a kind that is not found on Earth or in the Vedic iconography of this Goddess.

She stood there in perfect grace, her dark eyes filled with gentle radiance, divine sovereignty and higher wisdom.

I had learned her sacred mantras, and read her 1,000 holy names in the Lalita Sahashranama, but nothing had prepared me for this mystical encounter. And actually, my words fail to describe the love and safety you feel in the presence of a higher cosmic being.

The Goddess transmitted both bliss and peace, and for the first time, I entered the yogic state of "I am," with no awe, fear or separation. Instead, I felt the same as the Goddess.

She then took me on a tour of the galaxy, or perhaps different galaxies, because I remember entering several spiraling tunnels.

My encounter with Goddess Lalita happened in the city of Rameshwaram in South India, during a Yoga Nidra meditation, the "yogic sleep" in which you remain fully alert. Along with my Guru Dr. Pillai and many other students, I began meditating at 6 a.m. and we continued for hours.

I had always felt a connection with this Goddess, and when, in 2013, my teacher initiated me with the name Lalita, I immediately embraced it, adding it to my birth name and using it as a signature in all my work. I actually used a more powerful version of it—the Tamil name of this Goddess that includes the "th" sound: Lalitha.

I then learned that names and their sound waves influence your thoughts and create your life events. So a new name can change your life—especially a high-frequency name of the Divine.

Time Stopped

Have you ever experienced *missing time*? This happens when you lose consciousness of linear time as you would follow it on the clock in your everyday activities.

For example, you could experience 5 hours as a few minutes. In fact, my short voyage through the stars lasted only 20 to 30 minutes. But when the meditation ended, and we opened our eyes, I discovered that over 3 hours had elapsed between the beginning and end of the meditation.

In this time warp, Lalita and I entered what seemed like a spinning vortex of energy, a bluish, twirling tunnel filled with fluid pastel colors. Today I call this a *wormhole*—a term unknown to me at that time.

Then weightlessly, at the speed of thought, we traveled together to places I had never seen before.

Multidimensional Reality

As we traveled in space, Lalita showed me a geometrical design known in India as the Sri Chakra. Its shape encompassed the entire sky and was covered with luminous fog. In that space, I felt deep harmony, a complete lack of fear, and no thoughts.

"It's a hologram of the universe," the Goddess said telepathically. I simply stood there in bliss.

It was a huge silvery lotus shape, with countless triangles that appeared against a bright light, looking like a brilliant white smoke.

Strangely, I could observe the Sri Chakra in all its details with my 360-degree peripheral and rear vision, as if I had eyes everywhere in my body. But this enhanced ability to see in all directions seemed perfectly normal to me.

Then we entered the *"bindu,"* a shiny point in the middle of the Sri Chakra, whose spiraling energy pulled me in. It was like a vortex into which you fall, but at the same time, you are totally held and safe.

Many years later as I watched "Stargate," an old sci-fi series on TV, I recognized similar vortexes that took people to other worlds. You might be aware that many ex-military "whistleblowers" have revealed the existence of secret space programs, and stargates that look like spiraling holes, giving access to other galaxies.

As we were flowing into the Bindu gate, Lalita Tripura Sundari said that this point was a portal into other worlds and dimensions. It looked like a bluish, deep spiral. So, the Bindu was not a static point within a geometrical shape—rather, it was alive and conscious like an organic structure brimming with energy.

Apparently, the Goddess was initiating me into her secret tradition of Sri Vidya, a path to higher knowledge and her many other divine aspects.

Now I consider the Sri Chakra as the spaceship of Lalita Tripura Sundari. This Goddess is essentially a light being, who has no need for a physical vehicle, but she has the ability to take a physical body and incarnate into any form she wishes. She gloriously moves between worlds and dimensions instantaneously because she can be everywhere at once. I realized all this information intuitively.

As my consciousness on Earth was rooted in duality, I probably needed to experience space as a separate structure with its multiple aspects such as galaxies, wormholes, light, void, and luminous fog—all combined with the beauty of the Goddess and the Sri Chakra.

Nine years later, I still feel deep gratitude for this encounter, no doubt a gift from my Guru, who has been helping me with my spiritual growth.

On that day after this Yoga Nidra practice, none of the other students spoke of meeting Goddess Lalita. But I am certain that their experience corresponded to what they needed at that time for their evolution.

The Lalita Code

Lalita Parameshwari, or Supreme Goddess, embodies and reigns over the Sri Chakra, and deep within this sacred geometry are codes that can awaken the entire human race. In fact, according to many spiritual traditions, humanity is meant to ascend to the higher fifth and sixth dimensions, and even higher.

And despite her gentle and compassionate nature, the Divine Mother holds the power to control and hold together all the galaxies.

So, she is known by thousands of divine names—and these high-frequency sounds can raise you to a semi-divine state and bring you great miracles and transformation. Like the yogis of his Tamil Siddha lineage, my teacher believes that when you change your name, your karma and destiny will also change.

And I have experienced this positive transformation when I received the name Lalita, so I consider this a great truth. She is both Earth and all the galaxies simultaneously. In the Vedic tradition, she is the Supreme Goddess, pure, mystical, and the passionate wife of Shiva, the Supreme God.

Try This

- Take on a special or sacred name for some time. Watch for the miracles and positivity that this name might bring into your life.
- Think of the many people on Earth who reached high peaks of consciousness or achieved great positions in the world. They often adopted spiritual or illustrious names to signify their spiritual accomplishments.

For example, think of Mukunda Lal Ghosh, who became *Paramahansa Yogananda*, Sudhamani Idamannel, known as Amma or *Ammachi*, and Angelo Giuseppe Roncalli, who was *Pope John XXIII*, a truly saintly man.

Who and What Is Shakti

Shakti is the Goddess. Shakti is also the power of the sacred feminine in every woman and also present in men as love, compassion, and the power to protect the innocent, the Earth and all beings.

Our current new enlightened era—in its dawning stages—has been declared the "Shakti Yuga" or the Era of Goddess Power.

This apparently simple change is actually a monumentally positive shift that will transform the entire Earth plane—from a place of war, deceit and poverty to a magnificent planet filled with joy, love for our Source and each other, justice, abundance, and evolution.

According to the sages of India, Shakti is the *kundalini* power coiled at the bottom of the spinal column that can transform us into a God or Goddess when it rises to the upper energy centers or chakras.

Shakti is you. But shakti is also bliss (*ananda shakti*), ultimate desire that manifests with action (Iccha shakti), highest knowledge (jnana shakti), and ability to manifest anything (kriya shakti). So, Shakti is super-consciousness—omniscience, omnipotence, omnipresence—attainable for anyone who wishes to evolve to this higher state.

The Sri Chakra's Mystical Powers

The Sri Chakra embodies the union of Shiva Shakti—the entanglement of the sacred masculine with the sacred feminine, encoded in its beautiful design.

Feelings of deep love and well-being spring from the energy and vibrations of the Sri Chakra. In its presence in the cosmos, my consciousness and brain received streams of divine frequencies that stopped my thinking and temporarily deactivated the ego. I just felt open, peaceful, trusting, humble, and yet sovereign and divine.

We all become very attached to our ego identity, but it is ironic that we experience the best times in our lives when our ego is subdued—like when we fall in love, encounter the Divine, care for our children, form a deep friendship, or engage in a selfless deed to help others.

If you are skeptical about divine occurrences, it is normal as we all experience our ego as doubt and separation from the Divine.

Perhaps, it may help thinking that sound vibrations are the materials that build the universe. In physics, for example, the *string theory* speaks of the existence of many dimensions and frequencies.

Einstein, too, believed that everything in the cosmos is made of energy and vibration. So all the universes, living beings, stars, planets, and nature—everything—is made of frequencies, sounds and music, and so are you.

Out-of-Body Travel

The yogis of India and sages of Tibet can separate their consciousness from their physical bodies. In their out-of-body travels through the galaxies, they are able to communicate with higher beings. In these travels they have learned that the entire cosmos can be represented as vibrating geometrical shapes.

Not only have the yogis received cosmic wisdom on sacred geometry, but they have also used this knowledge to create buildings, temples, and *yantras*—or plates usually made of 5-metals or gold, radiating extremely positive energy.

These yantras are inscribed with codes and symbols that represent higher truths and secrets of the universe. Yantras are also encoded with sacred sounds and represent higher cosmic beings who can help you raise your consciousness.

So, the Sri Chakra is Lalita.

And yantras—like the Sri Chakra or Sri Yantra—embody spiritual science, material science, mathematics, and represent:

- The cosmos
- Elevated states of consciousness
- Higher dimensions or densities
- Power sounds
- Divine beings

With the higher frequencies from the Sri Chakra, you too can feel at one with all of creation, and the expansion of your consciousness will lead you to powerful thoughts that will create what you want.

Instead of being consumed with limited thoughts of your job, income, relationship, or another aspect of your life, you will become aware of your Goddess self—as pure love and immense power.

As the yogis say in Sanskrit, "*Aham Brahmasmi*" or "I am God." Your subconscious already knows the meaning of the holy Sri Chakra. However, by learning about its powers and experiencing the Goddess, you can awaken your full potential and activate the supernormal powers already existing within you.

For all these reasons, the Sri Chakra is considered the most sacred of all geometric designs and yantras.

The ancient sages have written about the abodes and characteristics of higher beings. For example, the *Soundarya Lahari*, the Wave of Beauty, is a famous ancient text that describes the Sri

Chakra in every detail. Written in 800 AD, it praised the perfect beauty of Lalita Tripura Sundari, the Divine Feminine, and a powerful force of creation. This text also declared that Shiva was inert without the shakti of his wife Lalita.

Technologies for Ascension

We all wish for an easier and more pleasant life. But we suffer from stress, negative emotions and unwelcome events.

Yoga Nidra is a divine gift from the omniscient yogis who gave us this technique to heal our body-mind and manifest our *sankalpa*.

A Sankalpa is your cherished desire that enters deeply into your subconscious and becomes your reality. So, the Sankalpa always manifests because you will create it in your life.

This profoundly relaxing technique can take you into a very deep meditative state in which your brain remains fully alert. Studies at Duke University, Yale and Harvard medical schools have pointed to the innumerable benefits of yoga Nidra for the body-mind—better sleep, increased calmness, clarity of thoughts, creativity, and well-being. But what science does not tell you is that Yoga Nidra can reprogram your subconscious to heal disease, manifest your intention, and help you experience spiritual growth.

Yoga Nidra is also very different from hypnosis—because, during its practice, you remain in full control of your consciousness at all times.

It was in this state of total clarity and alertness that I met the Goddess and learned that the Sri Chakra can lead you to spiritual enlightenment.

You could do some research and learn more about its nine interlocking triangles—five pointing downward and four pointing upward. Each triangle represents a different aspect of the universe, including the five senses, the five elements, and the five states of matter. However, these complexities will disappear as soon as you realize your own multidimensional nature, as happened to me.

A tridimensional version of the Sri Chakra, revealed by the yogis, looks like a pyramid. It represents a mystical mountain called the *Maha Meru* or Great Meru, known in many different spiritual traditions.

Lalita is believed to reside in this otherworldly pyramid.

Among other marvels, the traditional Maha Meru is said to host a wealthy city ruled by Goddess Lalita, who sits on a throne designed like a red lotus flower, rich with abundant precious metals and gems.

So, is Lalita an ET?

I am asking because I have heard accounts of a benevolent female extraterrestrial living under Mount Fuji—where there is an "arc" or mothership, and a city. So, an aspect of Lalita could be living under a mountain, where she reigns and operates ET technology.

Many people around the world are aware of other high-vibrational mountains on Earth—Arunachala Mountain, Mount Kailash, Mount Titicaca, and Mount Shasta, for example.

These are profoundly sacred spaces believed to be inhabited by higher cosmic beings. These evolved extraterrestrials have long been known as "Gods" because they are indeed millions of years more evolved than we are.

Once upon a time, these friends and protectors of humanity lived on Earth, but when the frequencies on our planet dropped due to the arrival of darker cycles, they lived interdimensionally in higher densities or dimensions.

Some went to live underground on Earth, maintaining a semi-physical form. In reality, the physical body can turn into light once a being evolves—which is also the predicted destiny for the human race at this time.

Many of these beings have left behind devices called arcs or conscious spaceships with extraordinary features and technologies. Other benevolent beings still live under these mountains. For me this is a more modern version of the stories of the Gods or Devas, the shining beings from the Vedic lore and other cultures.

LALITHA DONATELLA RIBACK

Divine Mountainous Homes

From my Vedic and yogic studies has transpired a very different history of Earth than what we have been taught in school.

The truth is that there are worlds in higher dimensions where more evolved beings live. I have learned that not only has Earth recently been liberated from some very evil ET groups, but that the entire planet is transforming into a higher form that will exist in the 5th dimension—and will vibrate much faster than its current third-dimensional version.

And when we live on a fifth-dimensional planet, we can more easily see and communicate with higher beings, which will be happening on Earth very soon.

We can ask for help from them, because they are both benevolent and available to assist us in our needs and evolution thanks to the law of *dharma*—meaning that just as each of us has a life purpose, so do they.

As for Goddess Lalita and her Maha Meru abode, could it be that there is an actual physical Maha Meru on the Earth plane? In fact, a Mount Meru really exists in Africa in the Arusha region of Tanzania—just west of Mount Kilimanjaro—and is one of the highest mountains in Africa.

All the above-mentioned mountains stand on powerful lay lines and are believed to host benevolent beings who exude love and compassion for humanity. Furthermore, I have read books by people affirming to be in communication with the so-called *Galactic Federation of Worlds*—a coalition of benevolent ETs who help populations that request assistance.

The human beings in touch with the ETs from this cosmic alliance have said that thanks to the positive changes happening in our Sun and our solar system, we will soon meet our brothers and sisters belonging to the Galactic Federation of Worlds.

These same extraterrestrials can also activate the spaceships and high-frequency devices present under the Himalaya and other mountains, in volcanos, and under the oceans.

The high-frequency devices or "arcs" can facilitate our rescue during catastrophic times. Myths—which are documentaries to me— also speak of civilizations that exist underground, like the *Telosians* under Mount Shasta.

Your Identity as the Goddess

Again, because your true nature is both perfect and divine, you are the Goddess, and she is you. So, you have inherited special access to her supernormal powers.

By raising your frequencies with meditation on a higher being like Lalita, you can acquire a light body and move through the galaxies at the speed of thought. As fantastic as this sounds, your transformation into a higher being happens through your choice, your commitment and a shift in consciousness—a quantum leap in evolution.

So, the Sri Chakra or Sri Yantra can help you change your timeline and recreate yourself entirely.

Try This

- Visualize or look at a Sri Chakra or Sri Yantra, research Goddess Lalita, talk to her.
- You can continue this meditation for as long as you wish. It is said that prolonged visualization of the Sri Chakra can help you acquire supernormal powers.
- Read about the Sri Chakra—its traditional descriptions reveal that here Lalita reigns uncontested over 64 other Goddesses known as Yoginis. These female deities are also adepts in both yoga and the arts of war, simultaneously honoring Lalita and fighting evil demons on her behalf.

Cosmology of the Sri Chakra and Maha Meru

One of the Yoginis or ETs in the Maha Meru is Goddess Varahi, the commander in chief of Lalita's fearsome army—which can destroy even the most powerful demons. Some scriptures even suggest that the Yoginis are not just 64, but a staggering *64 crores*—or 711 millions.

Another sacred, secret chant, the *Lalita Trishati*, describes Lalita as the Goddess worshipped by all the Gods, shining like a million suns, and creating galaxies with a single look. She wears the

Sun and the Moon as earrings, and through her glance she fulfills all the desires of her devotees, and destroys their sorrows and sins.

Similar to an NDE (Near Death Experience)

My vision and encounter with Lalita resembled a phenomenon called NDE in which a person leaves the physical body, travels through portals, and witnesses light, higher beings, spirit guides, attaining a deeper understanding of themselves and God. Although my body was fine and I did not die, I have had many similar experiences over the years.

I now believe that the Goddess can give you both wealth and enlightenment, simultaneously. She can help you embrace the perfect combination of material joys and ascension to a higher state of consciousness.

Shy and pure, Lalita was born from a fire ritual when the male Gods were unable to defeat some evil demons. She soon became the most powerful of all Goddesses—winning all battles against darkness with the help of the Yoginis, without engaging in battle herself, and always holding a gentle smile on her radiant face.

The Highest Shakti

The Goddess describes herself in these loosely translated verses from a hymn of the most ancient Veda—the Rigveda—called the "Devi Suktam":

LALITHA DONATELLA RIBACK

I am the sovereign Queen of the Universe, I give wealth to those who call on me. I am the all-knowing One, within the absolute focus on the highest. So the Gods have placed me everywhere, in countless energies, and numerous galaxies.

I created the sky, the space. I truly breathe myself forth like the wind, stemming out of and entering countless forms in all created worlds, beyond the heavens, beyond the world, so vast am I in my greatness.

So Lalita Tripura Sundari created space, and allowed life forms to grow and evolve.

Following are some of her countless divine attributes, forms and names, according to the scriptures.

- The Ageless
- Shodashi (eternally 16 years old)
- The Soul
- The Exhilarating
- The Noble
- The Wealthy
- The Graceful
- The Primordial Wisdom
- Mother of the Vast Universe
- The Shy
- The Goddess of Good Fortune

- The Lucky
- The Lovely
- Supreme Sovereign
- She who is surrounded by all Deities
- The Flawless
- The Goddess Bathed in Milk and Sandalwood
- The One Who Shines
- She Who is the Color of the Rising Sun
- Chintamani (gem of wish fulfilment)
- She who has a body like pure crystal
- Tripura Sundari, the most beautiful, most youthful, and most benevolent of all

Lalita's Love for Humanity and Her Desire to Save the World

During the global shutdown in 2020, my Guru performed an online fire ritual to invoke powerful deities to protect the world.

While chanting sacred mantras, he poured teaspoons of ghee and twigs into the fire. After invoking Ganesha, and Shiva's compassion, the time came to invoke Shiva's wife, Lalita Tripura Sundari.

My Guru pronounced her name out loud only once. Immediately, the sound of a loud explosion came out of the fire pit—

a sound I had never heard during a fire ritual. It vibrated powerfully like a bomb from a heavenly war against evil.

Visibly shaken, my Guru said: *"She is so upset."* The Goddess of love, compassion and the embodiment of Shakti, the fire energy itself and cosmic intelligence sent out her protest—and a warning to those responsible for the injustices and suffering of the human race.

And because this Goddess and her army always win and annihilate dark forces, the time for the liberation of humanity has come. A divine, higher energy has returned to the Earth plane. That explosion announced the upcoming new age of goodness—the Satya Yuga, the era of all truth, all-pervasive righteousness, widespread abundance, and spiritual ascension for all.

Coronation Day

Satya Yuga is the time when humans become royal, sovereign, free, wealthy, loving, and at one with the Divine. I believe that the time has come for humans to be coronated and acknowledge their own divine and powerful nature.

I once was coronated in a ceremony performed by my Guru. In fact, during a meditation invoking Lord Rama, an ancient divine king, I received an initiation and coronation. After receiving this initiation, I now belonged to the royal lineage of Rama, a form of Vishnu, an archetype believed to sustain and preserve the universe.

The Goddess now wants to coronate all humans. She reminds you of your royal beginnings, and the self-esteem coming from interacting with the Goddess is never based on ego or personality.

The current human royals can never attain the same state of self-confidence, as they rest their powers solely on ruling others, their material wealth, and the inevitable pride coming from ego-based fulfillment of desires.

On the contrary, at the time of Rama—the king who lived 35,000 years ago in India—royals were pure, loving, and prone to self-sacrifice in service to their people. They truly cared about humanity and the Earth Goddess.

Try This

Pick one or more of these rituals and recommendations to acquire incredible spiritual and mental powers. Your life will become filled with joy and positivity.

- Read the myths about Lalita. There are many today who believe that mythology is our true history. I believe this too.
- Buy a metal Sri Chakra yantra or a statue of Goddess Lalita. Then it will be easier to connect with the Shakti, power, beauty, purity, compassionate love of the universal Mother Goddess.
- Always shower before a ritual. Water Abishekam (hydration ceremony) to Lalita or the Sri Chakra is a most powerful ritual. Pour water on the statue, or yantra. Water is hydrogen (life) and an electrolyte, transmitting vibrations and

information. Because of the molecular structure of water, and the presence of hydrogen and oxygen, water is universally considered a means of purification and cleansing—and has long been associated with life and the Goddess.

- Milk Abishekam (Hydration Ceremony) to Lalita can bring you joy and pure thoughts—pure thoughts that manifest what you desire. Milk is nourishing and pure and pouring it on the Goddess' statue can bring you prosperity, beauty, and a loving relationship.
- Meditate on the Sri Chakra's divine geometrical yantra to visualize and embody the Goddess. Gently gaze at its sacred geometrical shapes for 5 to 10 minutes.
- Light a lamp of ghee, or a candle to her image or statue. Offer her a red flower—rose, hibiscus, or other. Ask for a special miracle.
- Thank her with the palms of your hands together in Namaste—acknowledge the sacredness of the light in yourself and her—feel her love, and smile.
- Always remember that you are divinely guided.

CHAPTER 2

THE DIVINE FEMININE IS LOVE

The Goddess is not merely a fertility deity, she is the muse, the inspirer of poetry, the inspirer of the spirit. -Joseph Campbell

The Goddesses are us in the future. Or you may think of them as unconditionally benevolent mothers, evolved ETs, Angels, or space sisters who love us deeply. According to many spiritual traditions, the Goddesses are more experienced and caring than we are at the moment—and if we so desire, they can be incredibly powerful friends who will help us reach our highest potential.

By connecting with them through our thoughts, our loving prayers, or with mantras that invoke them, you can easily summon them. So, imagine your prayers to the Goddesses as sending them an email or making a Zoom call with them.

Love is the Key to Cosmic Freedom and Bliss

Love is the glue that holds the universe together, and no other being can embody love better than the Goddess archetype. She is the Mother Creatress, the Protectress, the Divine Mother Goddess who will forever love you. We can find these same concepts in all cultures.

In the Indian tradition of Shaivism, love is considered God.

But even Shiva, the Supreme God, remains totally inert until Lalita—his consort—invites him to leave his meditation and dance the dance of creation with her.

Also, I believe that chanting Goddess mantras between 3:30 a.m. to 5 a.m. can uplift you so much that you might very well experience the 5th dimension—a higher density in which you become detached from the destructive, limited ego.

Then you can attain a higher state of wisdom in which there is only love, and you will identify yourself with the Divine. As the yogis teach, knowing that you are God is the main goal of your life on Earth.

GOLDEN AGE GODDESSES

As you experience higher dimensions of existence, you can manifest the life you want, embody deeper love, and be of service to others and to a higher cause.

The Goddess and Secrets of the Tamil Language

In the southern Indian state of Tamil Nadu, we find another Goddess: Angali, or the Universal Mother who is the most compassionate Goddess of all Goddesses.

She can remove the deep suffering plaguing so many people. She is both a form of fierce Kali and the highest wisdom Goddess Saraswati. You can ask her for protection from evil forces and supernormal powers by calling her name out loud with the word "Va", which means "come." *Angali Va.*

Repeat a few times this Tamil mantra, *Angali Va, Angali Va, Angali Va*, and notice your energy. Or try to chant this mantra for 30 minutes.

You may find that an emotion or memory will come up like a revelation, perhaps leading to a healing or a new understanding. The Goddess will respond to your call and provide anything you need, literally like a loving mother. This is the secret that south Indian yogis have held for eons—the Mother Goddess is the answer to all your sorrows. She is the One who brings true healing, pure love, and spiritual bliss.

So, Angali is the mother, a word that evokes love and nurturing in all languages. You will notice new positive ideas coming to your mind, you might experience a money miracle, or you will form a new, more loving relationship. Although Angali appears to be fierce to evil beings, she has a soft heart for good, righteous people. She also bestows incredible wisdom on her devotees.

The Tamil language, too, is said to carry the highest wisdom possible on the Earth plane. It is so powerful in its *nadham* or sound waves, that even a few words in Tamil can generate extraordinary energy that leads to miracles. This is because Tamil embodies both science and spirituality—which merge in Tamil syllables and words to form a divine language. So Tamil can transform your mind through its very high frequencies.

Also, the Tamil language is full of mysteries. What makes this language so special? Tamil has extraterrestrial origins.

In fact, the Pleiadian people from the Pleiades star cluster, lived on Earth one million years ago. They settled in the region of India corresponding today to the state of Tamil Nadu. They were responsible for seeding and nurturing life on Earth in those initial stages. Tamil is the language they spoke.

In addition, the Pleiadians deeply cared about this planet and all its life forms, especially the human race. And still today, they are said to be interested in the well-being of both humanity and Earth. And many humans today recall having lived a past life on one of the planets of the Pleiades.

Also, the Tamil language is unlike any other Indian language and can act as a spiritual technology to raise your consciousness, improve your thinking patterns, and bring you miraculous transformation.

Dr. Pillai has revealed that this language is very ancient and came to Earth from divine sources. "Tamil can make you a king. It is essential to approach Tamil as a science," he said.

When the human Pleiadian extraterrestrials arrived, they spoke the Tamil language—the only tongue spoken on the Earth plane then. The Pleiadians are considered both benevolent and loving and belong to one of the most evolved ET races in our galaxy.

According to Dr. Pillai, speaking or listening to sound waves from Tamil syllables and words can even remove your bad karma. Because karma is made of thoughts, Tamil words can restructure your brain and raise your consciousness—hence your life will improve.

So although Sanskrit mantras are very powerful in raising your consciousness, Tamil mantras are even more profound and work faster. And since everything is energy and vibrations, these divine sounds can catapult you into the experience of the Golden Age on Earth.

For example, a powerful Tamil name for Goddess Lalita is "Lalithambigai." These sounds are believed to generate much more power than the Sanskrit name "Lalita." So, calling on Lalita by the name Lalithambigai can raise your vibrations and connect you with the higher realms of the Goddess.

Another gentle and nurturing form of the Mother Goddess Lalita is Annapurna. Visualize a beautiful Goddess offering cooked rice to her husband, Shiva, and to the entire world's population. Rice is renowned in Ayurveda, India's ancient medicine, for its pure, deeply nourishing and cooling qualities.

The Goddess Can Help You in Practical Ways

We need the Goddess at this difficult time. -Dr. Pillai

So, we have seen that nourishing foods are associated with the Divine Mother Goddess, Annapurna, a form of Lalita Parameshwari. And in Vedic astrology, a form of the Moon called Soma is believed to heal all disease and make you like a God. The Moon is also connected with water, milk, rice, agriculture, all mothers, pure beauty, and femininity.

Moreover, we can connect with Goddesses in the plants and herbs we eat. In fact, we all have a natural pharmacy on Earth and within, as well as a healing nectar called "Amrita" that our brain secretes in higher, meditative states of consciousness and sometimes through specific yoga poses.

Healing guidance can come to you intuitively, and you will know exactly what to do to restore your health. However, the Goddess archetype can accelerate healing by raising your consciousness and increasing your wisdom and knowledge.

Growing up, my mother taught me that prayer can heal you. We often prayed to Mother Mary for various miracles, including healing. Also, at home we consumed an abundance of green vegetables and herbal teas with medicinal qualities. Detox in the springtime was a common practice in Italy, where I grew up. My mother often suggested eating lighter foods for healing purposes. I was naturally inclined to eat bitter greens—I loved them, and I would often say that I loved greens more than sweets. As a result, I enjoyed good health, and my skin had a glow, according to my friends.

My Healing Experience with a Goddess

"You have the cholesterol levels of an 80-year-old," said the doctor with wide eyes and a frown of disapproval. Sitting on the reclining chair in his office, I remained speechless. I was just 19 years old, and my thin body looked like a picture of perfect health.

I had moved out of my parent's home a few months earlier and given that I could cook nothing—not even an egg—I often opted for picking up croissants and creamy pastries nearby my home. Then I happily snacked on them throughout the day, except for an occasional outing to a restaurant or dinner at a friend's house.

My female friends would giggle at my bad dietary habits, or plainly criticized me. Also, they seemed to be in a permanent battle with their body weight and mostly nibbled on plain veggies.

On a good day, I would boil some pasta, dressing it with abundant butter and parmesan—the easiest way I knew for fixing a last-minute lunch. And since I was slender and did not suffer from acne or any chronic disease, I felt no motivation to change my eating habits—until that day, that is.

But now, in a state of panic, I thought about the threat of a heart attack or worse—death—unless I found ways to reduce my excessive cholesterol. Fortunately, the doctor did not prescribe any medication.

On my return home, I prayed to Mother Mary. I felt her compassion. Then I placed a huge volume of a medical encyclopedia—one of the few books I had brought from my parents' library—placed it on a table and searched for the word "cholesterol."

Then in a magazine I found a simple diet: eating daily a salad dressed with one teaspoon of olive oil. The article also recommended regularly consuming steamed green vegetables and avoiding heavy creams. All of which I did.

A month later, I visited the same doctor. He stared at me with great surprise, and waved the report of my recent blood test in his hand: "What have you done?" I nervously shifted my position on the chair. Then I asked in response: "What have I done?"

Finally, my doctor smiled, and said excitedly: "Your cholesterol is normal."

I said that I had followed a diet of green salads, carrots, and boiled artichokes. It turns out that these same foods are well known in Ayurveda—the incredibly effective medicine of ancient India. These vegetables can purify the liver, resulting in better sugar and fat metabolism. And it seems strange that such an easy protocol consisting of pure, cleansing foods cannot be found today on the list of doctors' recommendations.

Another Healing Goddess

Since 1993, I have studied and practiced Ayurveda, which treats the entire individual in his or her uniqueness. It addresses the body type, the season, the physiological needs, and the inborn tendencies of the mind—vivacious and enthusiastic, sharp and intellectual, or slow to learn but with great memory.

In a nutshell, these humors and tendencies of the body-mind can be summarized in three primary types: Vata or air, Pitta or fire, Kapha or earth-water.

And you might have already guessed it: there is a healing Goddess in Ayurveda. In fact, the Tamil Siddhas—a still existent 50,000-year-old lineage of ancient yogis who perform miracles—connect with this Goddess.

Her name is Ayur Devi, also known as the Empress of the Universe. These advanced yogis, masters of Ayurveda, meditate on Goddess Ayur Devi to receive healing and spiritual growth. They describe her as a beautiful Mother Goddess, and an embodiment of Ayurveda itself, with multiple arms and hands each holding a medicinal herb and spiritual tools.

As an aspect of Goddess Shakti, Ayur Devi is considered the Goddess of the Golden Age—known as the era of truth and enlightenment, Satya Yuga or Kritha Yuga—which is now back, and we are receiving the first glimpses of the fantastic changes it will bring into the world.

In my case, I trusted that both prayer and healthy foods could heal me, but I also decided that I wanted more physical exercise. So I increased the number of my weekly ballet and jazz dance classes. I also began running outdoors. As a result, I felt great.

You, too, can try to pray to a Goddess for guidance and healing. The Goddess can bestow upon you the knowledge of how to love and heal yourself. She reminds you that you are both sacred and miraculous, whether you are a man or a woman.

In addition, the Goddess embodies the Sacred Womb. Usually, women aspire to love, having harmonious relationships, beauty, and to helping others. Also, more often than men, women are compassionate, and in touch with their intuition, and most women carry a baby, sustaining life.

These qualities—more than science and technology—are life-enhancing and will protect humanity as we leave the dark ages, in which injustice, greed, exploitation and lies have reached the maximum level.

Although the Goddess and the feminine were suppressed for the last five thousand years—along with the knowledge of our divine origins—the power of the Divine Feminine has not waned. Rather, she still captures hearts and brings miracles to those who ask. She is the power of creation.

So, the Goddess is the queen of heaven, and she is here to heal the Earth plane through love and compassion. To remember our divinity, we need to remember her throughout the day, because the mind distracts us, putting us in a state of limited identity.

The Goddess will help you realize that you are royal, fully empowered and the embodiment of the perfect union of the Sacred Masculine and the Sacred Feminine.

A man is also a carrier of the Goddess archetype and her shakti power.

We are living in times of awakening and empowerment when righteous and God-loving people, who care about humanity, can experience their own inborn divinity and rise to the status of a human angel.

The good news is that you already carry the light and power of the Goddess. You are made of photon waves; you are a light being and can transform matter into energy and energy into matter—and the Goddess will teach you how.

She will uplift, protect and heal the entire world.

Moreover, the Goddess will put you in touch with your true emotions and intuition and connect you with the womb chakra—from where miracles originate—whether you are a man or a woman.

The Goddess Creates

The Goddess is connected with both the Creation and the kundalini—a coiled energy residing at the bottom of your spinal column.

With your meditation and yogic practices, like breathing exercises and yoga postures, you can activate this latent energy and make it rise to your upper chakras in the head, which will bring you supernormal powers.

The kundalini energy is also a Goddess—the feminine principle in its highest expression, and the ultimate feminine power, which has recently returned to Earth.

The higher frequencies now present on the Earth plane and the increasing photon light coming to our planet are due to an extraordinary—first time in a million years—upgrade of our solar system, which is part of the Divine Design, along with four main Earth cycles:

The Golden Age (Satya Yuga), the time of righteousness
The Silver Age (Treta Yuga)
Bronze Age (Dwapara Yuga)
Age of Destruction (Kali Yuga)

The end of the Kali Yuga is favored by positive galactic changes—happening both on the geophysical level and at the level of consciousness. This leads to the return of truth, the Golden Age and the Goddess Archetype, every time.

And it would be a mistake to consider the Goddess just an abstract idea, because she is real, an interdimensional light being, as well as an anthropomorphic being. She embodies the highest, pure form of intelligence that exists as potential within us. But this inborn intelligence needs to be activated through a connection with the Goddess.

So, the Divine Feminine can help you ignite the dormant, genius-like intelligence that exists within you. In fact, the Goddess also lives in an energy center or chakra that the yogis describe as a gold lotus—with one thousand petals found in your energy body, in the subtle brain.

It is also interesting to note that the yogis call your subconscious mind, *Chitta*, which is full of impurities, limitations from many incarnations and experiences that have brought you confusion and trauma.

But the Goddess embodies the highest, purest intelligence, the Feminine Divine Mind called *Chit*.

What is the Sacred Womb Chakra?

If you understand the feminine, you'll understand the secret of creation. The secret is in the womb. -Dr. Pillai

In the womb, matter and the soul merge and become one person. So, the Goddess—the higher woman, who is already in you—can empower you. When you become aware of her, she can activate all kinds of supernormal powers to heal you, and help you experience more love, attraction, protection and happiness.

CHAPTER 3

GODDESS BONA DEA AND HER SECRET POWERS

The Goddess does the work. The male God is a non-doer. But they are two sides of the same coin. One does not exist without the other. -Dr. Pillai

The smiling female florist handed me a headband studded with fresh pink roses. She had followed my suggested design, and I was happy with these small rosebuds. I stopped for a moment to admire this soft-rose creation. Then I tried on the headband and felt pleased by its lightweight and perfect fit. I paid the florist and left.

That evening, I placed the headband on my hair and wore it with a long, white silk dress with thin straps on my shoulders. Looking in the mirror I happily thought: *I really look like an ancient Roman.*

It was late spring of 2004 and graduation time at my school of yoga and enlightenment. The teachers were busy preparing a year-end party, and we students—all women—were invited to dress as a favorite Goddess.

I chose *Bona Dea*, the ancient Roman female deity of fertility and chastity, who protected women of all social backgrounds and ages. In addition, women who had undergone childbirth prayed to Bona Dea for healing their bodies and regaining strength.

She was a secretive Goddess, whose sacred name could not be spoken out loud. She was simply known as Bona Dea, Latin for *Benevolent Goddess*—and her full name is still unknown today. She was often associated with Venus, the Roman Goddess of beauty, love, and married life.

As I began to consciously embody Bona Dea, I was surprised by the fast transformation happening in me: I felt beautiful, self-confident, and even benevolent. For that evening I became her and all my thoughts, steps, gestures and spoken words began carrying her essence.

It turns out, in fact, that when you dress up as a Goddess and hold the intention of becoming her, staying open to her guidance, a magical alchemy will transmute your personality into a brighter and more charismatic you.

The yogis knew that the Divine is always within us, and we only need to refine our awareness to become conscious of our own divinity. "*I am you, and you are me*" say the yogis when they address the Divine. Or *Aham Brahmasmi*, meaning: I am Brahma, the Creator God. In ancient Hebrew this same principle is expressed as "*Eyeh Asher Eyeh: I Am That I Am.*"

For that entire evening, I felt as though I had always been Bona Dea and experienced her as a tingling in the body, feeling completely at ease, with a sense of invincibility.

I also observed the effects of dressing up as a Goddess on my classmates. In their divine costumes, they beamed a new fantastic energy, appearing ethereal. Everyone, including my favorite teacher, seemed to love my transformation, as I felt an expansion of consciousness, like some kind of quantum leap, leaving behind my old identity and the old ideas about myself.

That evening, accompanied by the sound of the crystal singing bowls, I entered a large room filled with flowers and animated schoolmates. At that same moment, another student was exiting the room, walking towards me.

As soon as she took a quick look at me, she immediately tightened her facial expression, turned her back and walked away in the opposite direction. My smile and greeting froze on my face.

In the heightened intuition springing from my new identity as Bona Dea, I had sensed a strong negativity coming from this person—and in the past, too, she had seemed irritated every time I spoke in class. I could not think of a reason for her strong dislike of me.

That night at the party she avoided me, and I ignored her without feeling any guilt or desire to pacify her.

Bona Dea was radiating her sovereignty through me, in addition to her strength and joy vastly beyond my usual capabilities. And it felt as though negative emotions had no power over me.

In the past, I had given extra attention or kindness when I sensed someone's dislike for me. I remember how many times I had tried to turn a person's hostility into friendship, but mostly in vain.

My yogic studies had increased my inborn compassion, and as a result, I had adopted a humanitarian outlook. So, more or less successfully, I would extend an olive branch to someone who treated me icily.

But this time, I reminded myself that I carried no responsibility for how others perceived me from their level of consciousness.

I was already an advanced yogi when I enrolled in the certification course, and my teacher showed respect for me and told me that she appreciated my 15-year experience with yoga. However, none of the other 20 students had prior knowledge of this subject before taking the course. Perhaps that woman resented my expertise.

However, thanks to Bona Dea's influence that night the woman's attitude did not bother me, and since I had not harmed her in any way, I simply put her out of my mind. And I loved my new sense of freedom.

All the other students looked inspired. I knew that like me they would soon be teaching the yogic path to evolution, as the great sages of India had taught. This new purpose seemed just so heavenly to me, worlds apart from my former work as a public relations executive, and the stress and disillusionment it had brought.

It was a splendid evening, and I made the resolution that my learning would never stop. I felt a deep desire for total surrender to the Divine Feminine and sensed the ever-present shakti permeating me.

Ancient Sacred Rites

After living in Rome for several years, I moved to the United States in my mid-20s. As I immersed myself in this new lifestyle with my American husband and our two children, I never thought of ancient Rome.

And yet, Bona Dea had suddenly arrived into my consciousness; I had embraced her presence and developed a desire to learn more about her. In my research, I found out that only her priestesses knew her secrets and true name. The sacred plants of myrtle used in her rites were considered so holy that the name of this plant, too, was sacred, and not commonly uttered.

Bona Dea held the title of *Laudanda Dea* or Admirable Goddess, and her spring and winter rituals were strictly reserved for women. In fact, she held a divine role in protecting all femininity, the hearth, virginity, and chastity. Female slaves, too, were allowed to worship her next to patrician matrons and the entire female population. While I absolutely condemn the use of slaves—male or female—this all-inclusive nature of Bona Dea made her a favorite of women from all social classes.

All Romans believed that Bona Dea's rituals held boundless spiritual powers that could protect the entire Roman Empire. For this reason, the diligent performance of her rites was meant to radiate good fortune in every aspect of Roman life.

The Shakti of the Goddess Fulfills Your Desires

Scriptures of India speak very highly of the Shakti, the enormous powers of the Goddess. Rituals to her are believed to yield very positive results, even miracles. Many times I have experienced the positive effects of such rituals.

I am aware that many consider miraculous occurrences fruits of "placebo." Yet a placebo showcases our ability to harness psychological, emotional and spiritual energies to heal ourselves.

Although Bona Dea's full name was never identified, we know about her powers of divination—channeled by her priestesses—who conveyed to the authorities and adepts the Goddess' higher wisdom, knowledge, and predictions of future events. In addition, Bona Dea was also venerated for her miraculous healings.

According to Roman author Cornelius Labeo (3rd century AD), many people considered Bona Dea the same as Earth, Terra, Maia, or the Great Mother, whose name reminds us of the Vedic Goddess *Maya*, who is Lakshmi, the Goddess of wealth and abundance.

However, unlike the festival of the Roman Goddess Maia that was open to everyone, Bona Dea's rituals were strictly forbidden to men and could only be performed by selected priestesses, including the Virgin Vestals—highly trained and educated women, who also officiated the rites of *Vesta*, the Goddess of the sacred fire, home, and family.

In ancient Roman statues, paintings, bas reliefs and coins of Bona Dea, she appeared alternatively as a gorgeous young woman, an attractive and dignified matron, or a married woman holding a scepter and a cornucopia, symbols of power and abundance. Moreover, the Goddess was sometimes depicted with a snake, likely representing pure sexual energy, fertility, protection, and ultimate transformation.

Similarly, in the Vedic culture, the snake represents the power of the *kundalini*, the immense spiritual energy coiled at the base of the spinal column, as we saw earlier.

The ancient Romans feared any obstacle in the rites of Bona Dea—because they understood the Divine Feminine as the great power that sustained the Empire's wealth, protection, happiness, and life itself.

In India, too, a myth tells the story of Lakshmi, the Goddess of wealth, who once left her husband's heaven called Vaikunta. Immediately after her departure, heaven was devastated and *Indra*, the king of the Gods, lost his monumental, good fortune. This episode beautifully showcases the huge power attributed to the Goddess across cultures and eras.

An Early Sign of Decadence of the Roman Empire

Although Bona Dea's festivals were highly respected in Roman society, in 62 B.C. a terrible scandal caused by a man's mischief, tarnished the secrecy and mystery of this Goddess' rites. This was perhaps a sign that darker times were dawning for the Goddess religions in the West.

The man's name was Publius Claudius Pulcher, a Roman patrician and influential politician notorious for his many sexual indiscretions and frequent violations of Roman law. Apparently, once he even tried to seduce his own sister—and her husband relentlessly chased Publius Claudius across Latium, the region of Rome, to kill him—but did not succeed. Publius Claudius escaped and left Rome.

When he returned to public life years later, he became infatuated with Pompeia, Julius Caesar's second wife, and in an attempt to seduce her, he dressed up as a woman. He then crashed the winter festival of Bona Dea—a well-guarded event during which all males, even male animals, were strictly banned.

But he was quickly recognized and exposed by Caesar's mother, also attending Bona Dea's rites. This unprecedented violation of Bona Dea's sanctity and seduction attempt led to Julius Caesar's divorce from Pompeia. Likely Caesar was incensed, and to preserve his reputation and political standing he repudiated his wife. Yet Claudius' sacrilege was followed by little consequence, thanks to his strong political allies.

Unfortunately during the early Christian era, the myth of Bona Dea was banned and ultimately lost. But Joseph Campbell, a great expert of archetypes, said that *a God or Goddess cannot be killed*. Instead, their divine influence will live on, becoming even greater when their myth goes into hiding.

To this day, Bona Dea lives in the collective unconscious, and remains one of my favorite Roman Goddesses. Also through my intuitive insights, I have learned that she is again active here on the Earth plane.

It Has Already Happened

In 2018, after praying to a favorite Goddess, I invested a considerable amount of money in a media event that could help me scale my business. I also signed up for a VIP event with my business coach. The most important reason I joined the VIP group was: the bonuses included a one-on-one call with a prominent media person

I had been trying to reach. I felt great satisfaction having secured a Zoom call with this person.

The VIP event came and went, with no sign of my appointment with the media person. After a month without hearing from my coach's team—I emailed them to inquire about the scheduling.

Here is their reply: "*Lalitha we apologize for the confusion. The call with [name of media person] was part of a lottery that will be drawn tomorrow. The consultation with her was not included in the ticket you paid for the VIP event.*"

Upon reading these words, I felt a tightening in my chest. My thoughts became super negative from the shock:

A lottery among 500 attendees? But I don't believe in lotteries! I even detest the Lotto. And the rare times I paid for a lottery ticket I didn't win anything.

I realized I had a deep-seated belief that I would never win anything. But it was a simple belief—which could easily be changed. For example, I had always received beautiful and even luxurious gifts and had no problem accepting that my family and loved ones enjoyed giving me beautiful things. But I had never tried to shake my doom-and-gloom thoughts about winning lotteries, because I had never paid attention to it.

Two days later, I received another email from the same staff. It said: "*Congratulations, Lalitha! You won a 1:1 call with…*[name of the media personality]."

This time I almost fell off of my chair from the excitement. I was overjoyed, especially because, for over 24 hours, I had been certain I would never get that prized call. When I regained my composure, I received a fulgurating insight. In fact, I have never forgotten this—I had just remembered the real secret of successful manifesting.

How Did It Happen?

Soon after remembering this manifesting formula, I realized that the yogis, too, employ this same method to help their students. And you can apply it to anything you desire.

Think of it this way: for an entire month, I had no doubt that I had secured a call with that well-known media personality. I would also fantasize about all the benefits stemming from her guidance—like publishing a great guest article or landing an interview in a top media. So many more people would learn about my work, I could help a lot more clients, spread happiness, and be rewarded with great financial gains—and so on.

After all, I thought I had bought that privilege with the event ticket. Most likely, my intuition and subconscious knew that I would win the lottery, but my rational mind "misunderstood" the conditions for receiving the 1:1 call. Also, I had fallen into bitter disappointment, but only for 24 hours, fearing that I would never win that lottery.

Let us do the easy math: 30 days of certainty minus one day of fear = 29 positive days of certainty that I had achieved my goal of meeting with that journalist.

Can you see the power of 29 days full of trust and happiness from the fulfillment of your desire?

This is what countless spiritual masters, including Jesus, have told us. Even the gnostic Gospel of Thomas said that to manifest you need to believe that you have already received what you want. Believe that you have already received the answer to your prayer. We wonder why this gospel was left out of the canonical texts.

So, faith and imagination are important—and if you have no faith, the fastest way to manifest is by asking the Goddess—who is both your Mother and your own higher self. Then, imagine that your desire has already been fulfilled by the Goddess, and this will eliminate any doubt or ego that can kill miracles before they happen.

Try This

- Visualize your desired outcome with love and trust. You might experience a "quickening" in your body—a sense that you are no longer flesh and blood and that you are expanding. You may also feel deep joy for your desired accomplishment.
- Imagine in details the happiness you feel for having received what you want, and the benefits that will follow when you have reached your special goal.

Ask the Goddess for a Special Miracle

Maybe you *don't give a fig* about media people and publicity, but I am sure you have a great desire for an experience or a cherished dream in your heart. It can be as huge as becoming president of your country, or a simple two-week vacation that your bad finances have not allowed so far.

For example: Imagine that you already have the car you want—and ignore the thought that its price makes it unattainable for you. In your consciousness, you have already bought it. It has already happened, and the car is already in your garage.

Even if you have no garage, know that the car is now parked outside your home. The pleasant emotions that flow from this imagination are well worth the effort—and even if you do not receive that car, you have already experienced some joy from the imagination of owning the car.

Moreover, my experience has been that the Mother Goddess always fulfills her children's wishes, one way or another. So just keep focusing on the car, or relationship, or job, or sum of money you wish—with full faith, and you might very well receive it.

Bona Dea's Miracles to You

She is a universal well-wisher and can fulfill your desires for wealth and royalty consciousness. In addition, she can bless you with progeny if you want children, and bring you relationship happiness with your loved ones, ensuring that your home embodies love, safety, and emotional and physical nurturing. Also, she can grant you an aura of pure beauty, luster and perfect health.

First and foremost, pay attention to how you feel when you see images of the Sacred Feminine. In fact, evolved beings like the Goddesses—who can also be called evolved female ETs—emanate a larger field of light and colors indicating higher frequencies, invisible to eyes.

Also, the Goddess teaches you to love yourself and your uniqueness, and can help you expand your own auric field—or the halo of energy that surrounds your body, as Kirlian photography shows.

Try This

- Choose an aspect of the Divine Feminine and connect with her. Dress like this Goddess, research about her, and speak to her frequently. Trust that she can hear you and may respond through emotions, dreams or events. Do this for at least one month, or ideally for 45 days.
- If you can find a picture of your chosen Goddess, try to have it laminated or buy her statue, if available. Offer some fruit, a small chocolate, a lit candle and incense to her image—this will create a bond of trust and intimate communication.
- Ask her for what you want and "feel" that it has already been fulfilled.

- Offer as many flowers as possible to an image or statue of the Goddess—she could be Mother Mary, Lakshmi, Tara, or Saraswati. Flowers embody *Akasha*, the pure space element.
- Because flowers originally came from another galaxy, as the yogis have revealed, surrounding yourself with flowers and offering flower petals to a divine being takes you beyond space-time. Speak your prayer out loud into a flower. The power of your prayer will multiply at least 100 times.
- When you receive your miracle, always acknowledge it—even if it is a small one. Express your gratitude to the Goddess aloud or mentally.
- Smile often when you pray. Your body will then release feel-good hormones that include serotonin, dopamine, and endorphins. In this positive state of gratitude or joy, it is much easier to contact and connect with the Divine and experience positive life changes.
- ***Golden Light Meditation:*** Visualize yourself in front of the Goddess, facing her. See two beautiful beams of golden light leaving her eyes and entering your eyes. Your eyes now are filled with golden light and golden hues. Then, a golden beam of light coming from the center of the Goddess' forehead and from her third eye enters your forehead and fills your third eye. You now are at one with the Goddess' essence. Feel your beauty, power and pure energy come alive. You are the Goddess.

- Pray for what you want. Trust that she hears your prayers and always responds. Ask her. She is your Mother and wants you to be happy, beautiful, loved, and respected.
- Always hold the awareness that the Goddess is in you, and you are in her because it is true. Open your heart and become fully empowered with your identity as the Goddess.

CHAPTER 4

VESTA, THE GODDESS OF FIRE AND THE HEARTH

In Satya Yuga, suffering will cease to exist, and people will live lives of luxury, devoted to God and ascending to higher levels of consciousness. And the Goddess will rule this new age. -Dr. Pillai

Sitting on my heels, forehead glued to my rubber yoga mat, I felt a deep relaxation spreading throughout my body. I was holding the *Balasana* or Child Pose. A pleasant sense of surrender followed, and I remained completely still.

The tension in my muscles and fatigue from the long hours of yoga practice quickly dissipated, and I enjoyed that feeling of letting go, like when you have nothing else to do.

But unexpectedly, deep fear and sadness surfaced, followed by vivid images behind my closed eyes. I began to cry and tried to hide it from the other yoga students. I mentally wondered: What's going on?

The images I saw in my mind's eye included the ancient Roman Forum and the House of the Vestals—not as today's ruins in Rome, but rather as they must have looked 2,000 years ago.

Everything from the shining white marble buildings to the garden and the paved roads, it all appeared perfectly new. The manicured grounds with lovely bushes of white and pink oleanders, the white columns and the immaculate temple dedicated to Goddess Vesta all stood in pristine magnificence, bathed in the afternoon sun. And yet, after seeing all this, I felt scared.

Then I saw myself dressed in a white tunic—or rather, I knew that the girl I was looking at was me. The tunic suggested that I belonged to the ancient Roman order of virgin priestesses, the Vestals. I knew all this without thinking. Everything seemed opulent, even elegant.

And, in recent research, I learned that the House of the Vestals as I saw it in my vision, had been restored and made more luxurious on the command of Octavian, a Roman emperor also named Caesar Augustus.

The House of the Vestals was close to the emperor's Regia, the imperial palace, visible just behind the temple. Both he and his wife Livia, as I recently read, were fervent devotees of Vesta and gave more prominence and concessions to the Vestal priestesses.

These facts explain why, in my vision, the Forum appeared incredibly luxurious. At that time I honored and served the Mother Goddess, Vesta, and I cared for the eternal flame that protected the Empire. Again, in that vision, I saw myself looking young, sad, and frightened.

I knew intuitively that I was facing a possible execution, and I instantly recalled that I had broken my chastity vow. I saw the color of my hair, my large brown eyes, and a shocked expression on my pale face.

My Yogic Studies

This vision happened in 2003, when I was enrolled in a yoga certification program at a school in the state of Ohio, USA.

Two female teachers, and an orthopedic doctor from the Cleveland Clinic, our anatomy instructor, taught us classes in a large building on the campus of the Ursuline College, run by Roman Catholic nuns.

The school's sunny interiors were unlike typical classrooms and broke away from the monotony of common university buildings. In fact, this campus was beautifully kept and displayed abundant green trees, lovely shrubs, vast green lawns, a Japanese stone garden, and even an outdoor labyrinth made of medium-height boxwood walls.

I also loved the adjacent yoga boutique, where I shopped for heart-shaped crystals and other meditation items. I really enjoyed this university's mystical atmosphere and its palpable divinity.

A year before my graduation, I took a 4-hour yoga asana class, with poses that lasted a bit longer than usual. At the end of the class, my intentions were to achieve a deep relaxation and refresh my body-mind through the Child Pose.

And that is when my third eye opened, and I saw ancient Rome and myself. I knew that all Vestals took the vow of celibacy, and I realized from my feelings that had broken this oath.

Goddess Vesta and her sacred flames were at the heart of every Roman household. Like Hestia, her Greek counterpart, Vesta was a virgin Goddess, and her chastity and purity were considered a protective energy that ensured safety, well-being and continuity of the Roman Empire and its populations.

For *Ovid*, the celebrated Roman poet, Vesta embodied the Goddess of Fire. Her rites included fire rituals and chanting diligently performed by the virgin Vestals, who also ensured that the sacred flame at the center of the temple's hearth would burn 24 hours a day. Failure to do so would result in punishment, followed by extensive ceremonies to repair the spiritual damage caused by the extinguished flame.

The people's love for Vesta was so widespread throughout Rome that even Ovid praised her as the Mother Goddess of all

Romans. He also called her "the Earth Goddess"—known as *Tellus* in Latin.

"*Vesta and Tellus are the same Goddess,*" he wrote, further praising her as the "first" among all Gods: "I*n praying, we address Vesta first, who holds first place.*"

The following verses, too, reveal Ovid's deep devotion and love for the Goddess:

Vesta equals Earth. Sleepless fire underlies both. Earth and hearth denote their own fixity. Earth is like a ball resting on no support, a great weight hanging in the air beneath. Its very rotation keeps the globe balanced. (Ovid, Fasti, Bk 6, 9 June)

Apparently, the ancient Romans knew that the Earth was both spherical and as hot as fire below its surface—information we have only recently acquired in 2023, when scientists discovered a molten layer beneath the Earth's mantle.

So, Mother Vesta, like the Earth, contained an internal fire that sustained and gave life. For the Romans, Vesta existed both in the living flame on her altar and in the purity of her priestesses. These divine Vestal girls and women channeled Vesta's royal voice, chanting: "*I am the one who is. No man can see my form through my veils.*"

I knew that the Vestals were prophetic priestesses who communicated with the Goddess, predicting future political, social, and economic events in the Roman Empire.

The Forum's Beauty

A sequence of memories from my ancient Roman life became juxtaposed with a sense of doom from discovering that I risked being executed.

On the one hand, the Forum was incredibly beautiful, and I could feel its divine energies, see the lush gardens, and the buildings' polished, white marble reflecting sunlight in that fateful afternoon. I can still see the green shrubs surrounding the garden. Perhaps this memory is one of the reasons for my love of the green-white color combination. Today I still surround myself with décor and clothes in this color scheme.

On the other hand, I still feel the fear of finding myself alone in that garden. I can almost smell the white oleanders and chasteberries near the temple of Vesta. A tense energy pervading the temple grounds and the flowers' nauseating scent still linger in my mind.

They say that smell, more than all the other senses, can swiftly take you back in time. Today, the smell of oleanders still causes me nausea and takes me back to ancient Rome in one whiff.

In my vision, the garden of the Vesta temple provided me with much-needed support as I awaited my fate. Shivering despite the warm sunlight, I leaned against the white marble wall. I could see and feel on my back the ornamental molding made of protruding horizontal strips.

These clear, detailed images proved to me that time does not exist. I was reliving, in fact, each sight, emotion, perfume, action and sensation of that day in ancient Rome.

The temple's haunting beauty was a far cry from today's ruins in the Roman Forum. How sadly dull it all looks now in its dusty surroundings. A newer, darker reconstruction of the temple with travertine columns has replaced the original immaculate and polished marble.

My visions of this place—no matter how far-fetched they seemed at first—were later confirmed down to their most minute details and reflected historical records from my research.

Successive Events

Suddenly, in my vision, I saw my beloved. I was already aware that he and I had been accused of meeting secretly beyond the gardens of the temple complex. This simple act was considered a violation of my chastity vow. In reality, nothing much had happened between us. But we had met several times while the older Vestals protected our secret.

I saw him, a youth my age, wearing a white tunic. Intuitively I knew he was a Pretorian guard of the Pontifex Maximus, Caesar

Augustus. Then, more recently, new visions came, and more intuitive information engulfed me while writing this book.

But soon I began to doubt the accuracy of these new visions. For example, there are no traces of white marble in today's Forum—I know this because I used to live in Rome, and the temple had always appeared to me as a very desolate place.

After a quick online search and reading several books by historians and archeologists, I learned that the temple underwent demolition after 1549 AD, when all the white marble was taken away to be used for the construction of the Pope's palaces. My heart still sinks for such audacity that violated the sacredness of Vesta's temple.

Earlier, other rulers had desecrated the temple and neglected all the provisions left by the second king of Rome, Numa Pompilius. In fact, before he died, he had ordered the construction of a huge marble container to store books about the Goddess religions—along with accurate instructions for Vesta's rituals.

But at his death, some senators inspected the books and found their contents to be too "dangerous," and ordered the books' destruction. So, the Goddess religions faced suppression, just so senators and emperors could maintain their own sacerdotal and political powers.

I find that to be so unfair. And it is heartening to think of today's renewed focus on the Goddess archetype and Divine Feminine on a global scale. The Goddess will be the hallmark of a Golden Age, putting an end to millennia of crimes against women and the suppression of Goddess religions in the West and Middle East.

More About My Spontaneous Past-Life Memories

While holding the Balasana pose on my yoga mat, I also received other visions. I was standing in the garden adjacent to the House of the Vestals, where I lived. I noticed the green shrubs and inhaled the unpleasant smell of white oleanders. My stomach turned, and I felt petrified with fear.

In my mind's eye, I saw my beloved again. His image did not bring me feelings of love or joy but rather even deeper emotions of fear. I had probably suffered so much due to my connection with him that I barely wanted to look at him.

The more I typed these memories onto the pages on my computer, the more my mind was triggered to recall new details. Non-stop visions began coming like continuous water drops from a broken faucet.

The ancient Roman version of me held a desolate facial expression, and I began feeling the unbearable responsibility and sorrow weighing down on her young shoulders. It was as if it were happening to me in real-time.

As a Vestal, I had promised to maintain an immaculate reputation, and my transgression was considered harmful to the Roman Empire. Moreover, there was a collective belief that the

Vestals' virginity increased the power of the rituals and ensured Rome's perpetual connection to the Gods.

By breaking my vow of celibacy, I had automatically put my life in danger because a priestess found guilty of this crime was buried alive—as the law strictly prohibited killing a Vestal. And because spilling her blood was also forbidden, burying the girl alive was considered an acceptable compromise.

I saw my ashen face as I waited, thinking of my upcoming death and expecting the guards to come and arrest me at any moment. While I observed myself standing outside the *atrium Vestae*, I could see my paralyzing fear in the stiffness of my spinal column and limbs.

But what was the reason for these visions? I still did not know. After all, my yoga practice always left me calm and refreshed, and these images of ancient Rome seemed particularly nonsensical, as I had been living in the United States for many years.

In this life, when I lived in Rome as a young adult, I simply accepted that I disliked the Vesta Temple. I never visited it, although it was located a mere 10-minute drive from my apartment near Piazza Navona. And Vesta's temple is still considered today an enchanting place of great beauty and mystery.

Moreover, in the spontaneous memories of that previous life, I felt great love and veneration for Goddess Vesta. Also, while writing this book, I remembered another event in ancient Rome when I was just six years old.

Against my will, my parents had left me with the temple's authorities, and I sat stunned and tearful in the House of the Vestals. I had just undergone the rituals of initiation performed by the elder Vestals and the Pontifex, but I could not recall the ceremony. In research, I learned that this initiation included cutting the little girl's hair, before the wearing of the veil.

My father had tried to appear detached, without any trace of love for me, perhaps to avoid a public display of emotion. My mother, too, had seemed indifferent to my departure from my parental home.

Yet I was certain that both my parents loved me, even though they had chosen prestige and status over love and decided to force me into priesthood. A Vestal daughter, in fact, was considered to bring much luster and fame to a Roman family, even an illustrious one like mine.

In my research, it was confirmed that most Vestals belonged to Patrician families, who considered it a great honor for their daughters to serve the Goddess. After the initial ceremonies, the little girls would move into the House of the Vestals and were later trained to become priestesses.

From my intuitive insights, I remembered that in my teens, I began performing all the sacred rituals to Vesta—for the protection of Rome and the Empire.

After the initial ceremony, I cried and longed for my mother and my home.

I knew that the Vestals' powerful ceremonies would keep all misfortune and disease at bay, and the eternal fire on the altar would burn brightly at all times, day and night.

Despite my initial dislike for the new surroundings, I soon adjusted to this new life, and I happily performed the daily tasks: I studied the scriptures and learned how to invoke Vesta's blessings. And I especially enjoyed learning the invocations to the eternal flame. All this knowledge came in less than a second. Also, during the writing of this book, new visions and information came very fast.

It seemed as though the Goddess had become my real mother. Consecrated to her cult, I vowed to abstain from marriage and avoid any interactions with men, except for the Pontifex Maximus—who was like a father figure.

And I understood early on that transgressing the vow of chastity implied the capital punishment for both the Vestal and her lover. In what follows are some more recent visions.

In my earlier recollection in the yoga studio, I appeared to be 18 years old. I feared for my boyfriend's life, but I had some hope that we would be pardoned. In fact, intuitively, I knew that in the past, several Vestals had been absolved, despite an initial verdict of guilt.

Again, as I stood outside near the temple awaiting judgment, I remembered the short trial, which was a mere formality. The authorities of the temple had removed the white veil from my head, now bare, banning me from entering the temple. I felt impure and lost in a myriad of emotions.

Every time I chose to, I could see myself. Loose bangs of hair framed my pale face, pretty in its delicate, girlish features. My chestnut braids were still twisted into a bun atop my head.

I also saw my beloved in my mind's eye. I noticed his handsome face, the dark brown curls falling on the forehead. When I had first met him, I understood from his insignia that he belonged to the elite army of the Emperor.

I felt no guilt for our connection, as my love for him was sincere and devoid of sinful motives. In fact, a vague sense of injustice haunted me—as I knew that some other Vestals, too, secretly met with their lovers in the middle of the night. The elder Vestals had protected us all from being exposed. But a jealous lictor guard, whose advances I had refused, alerted the authorities.

On the yoga mat with my eyes still closed, I again saw my Roman boyfriend—probably as a memory of his secret visits to the Forum. I saw his good-looking face framed by curls and his white tunic.

Awakening to Deeper Realities

As regards my intuitive visions, since my childhood they have happened without any prompting from me. But more recently, I began receiving extraordinary results by intentionally projecting my consciousness into the past. I then saw accurate historical events as detailed images in mind.

This process works something like when you wonder what happened to you a day earlier. You may think: *What did I do yesterday?* Soon memories of your previous day will begin coming to your mind: faces of people you met, activities you engaged in, a particularly deep emotion you experienced, the foods you ate, or a fulfilled desire.

Recently when I engaged in a kind of "remote viewing" of my ancient Roman life, I learned that my boyfriend and I had met in Rome during the festival of Vesta. I still felt and heard the excitement pervading the streets of Rome, filled with celebrations, prayers, and countless people flocking to the Vesta temple during this holiday.

When he and I looked at each other for the first time, I was wrapped in a virginal white garment and wore a ceremonial veil on my head. I instantly fell in love—and blushed while he continued to stare at me. Accompanied by two other Vestals, I entered the temple and realized that he was one of the praetorian guards of Augustus Octavian, the emperor and Pontifex Maximus, who presided over the sacred rituals to Vesta.

Despite the extremely close supervision, my beloved and I were able to meet for a few weeks without being caught, until that mean-spirited guard reported us to the Pontifex.

In the garden, weak in the legs, I now trembled at the memory of the shameful trial, during which I had kept my eyes closed, chin down, feeling my aching chest. Then, after the removal of the sacred white veil, I was taken back to the House of the Vestals.

For some mysterious reason, after the sentence, neither the judge nor the soldiers carried out the prescribed flogging. Were they perhaps afraid of my parents' political connections and high status? This I cannot remember.

This unexpected good fortune led to my hope that my life would be spared. I knew that many condemned Vestals had later been absolved—most likely due to the intercession of their prominent families, as the emperor took into serious consideration political pressure from patrician clans.

Recently, while reading a description of the Atrium Vestae—and the living quarters of the Vestals I was assailed again by hidden fears and a strong sense of nausea, and I could even smell the food in the dining areas. And although the Atrium was a beautiful construction with frescoes on its walls, lovely mosaic floors, and surrounded by impressively tall columns—even the thought of living there brought me shivers.

Returning to my intuitive memories of that day standing outside the Atrium Vestae awaiting punishment, I can still feel my terror, tears, and a wish to see my parents, even though I was certain that they did not approve of me. I also knew that an attempt to escape would be futile, as groups of lictors would be sent out to capture me.

My boyfriend was being held in a different building, not far from the temple. His status as a Praetorian had allowed him access to many privileges, but as a man he had broken the law by entering the temple grounds, as this was allowed only when he accompanied the emperor during the Vestalia festival.

When our indiscretion was discovered, my boyfriend appeared to be my same age, about 18 years old. He was immediately stripped of his military distinction, and like me he awaited the final decision of the court.

I really hoped that Caesar Augustus would spare his life. Again, like a flashback, I saw my boyfriend near me by the same white marble building. He was wearing a plain white tunic.

While writing this chapter of the book, I attributed his white tunic to a mistake of my imagination. In fact, I believed that the Praetorians wore red tunics, gold insignia, and red helmets. But during my research, I discovered that praetorian guards commonly wore white tunics or cream-colored *togas*.

As I read this information that confirmed my vision, I had tears of recollection and entered a state of deep sadness.

Later another doubt made its way into my mind. Remembering my vision of this young man, I began thinking that my assessment of his age must be wrong. I reasoned that a praetorian guard, expert in martial arts and war tactics, could not possibly be recruited at age 18. But my vision was clear: my boyfriend was my same age.

So, I persisted in the research until I read: *"Praetorian guards were recruited between 15 and 32 years of age."* So, I stopped doubting and henceforth accepted my visions and recollections as true.

I am aware that the rational mind has the uncanny habit of resisting intuitive knowledge, trying to debunk it. Also, it may seem extraordinary that my memories should still be so vivid.

Perhaps, the clarity of my visions can be compared to those of individuals undergoing a Near Death Experience or NDE—during which a person can clearly remember a visual sequence of events in their smallest details—even decades later.

For example, many accounts of NDEs report that experiencers can remember:

- Floating outside their physical bodies
- Clear images of light and light beings
- Receiving revelations of their life path and purpose
- Meeting departed ancestors and spiritual guides
- Their past lives
- Revelations on the nature of time and space
- And so much more

The clarity of these images remains unchanged even many years after the NDE, whose spiritual meaning becomes more apparent and integrated with time.

I now realize that my past-life memories of being a Vestal came during that yoga class to reveal an unhealed wound from the past—a terrible trauma connected with religion. And in that light, it is no surprise that the visions surfaced just as I was beginning my teachings of ancient spiritual practices.

Subconscious suffering can inhibit the full expression of our spiritual being. So spontaneous memories of past lives occur to bring healing, and deeper awareness.

Only after this integration of our soul's needs, can we become whole and able to share our talents and gifts with the world. And helping others on their spiritual paths was definitely part of my life purpose.

More Channeled Information

Intuition or non-local awareness from "Akashic records" delivers knowledge or information you have not studied or received from a book or another person. This knowledge will be embedded in your mind and consciousness, or it might come to you in the form of words. Or you might see in your mind's eye images containing some revelations.

Occasionally, dreams, visions, or literally spoken words from an external voice will bring you knowledge from your soul.

What I recommend, though, is to stay very alert, because if you hear negative thoughts that are demeaning or hurtful to you, like bad words, or judgmental and cruel thoughts—these might come from the ego, or from beings who are not from God.

So, you need to ignore such thoughts or words. Replace them with a prayer or pure mantra like "OM." Or say out loud a few times a name of the Divine Mother like Durga, or the Divine Father—like *Krishna, Shiva,* or *Jesus.*

For example, you can say out loud or think:

Jesus, Jesus, Jesus
Krishna, Krishna, Krishna
Shiva, Shiva, Shiva
Durga, Durga, Durga

Choose one of these holy names and ask this being to remove negativity and darkness in your life or in a particular situation. As a matter of fact, names of divine beings are very powerful and positive sounds that can vanquish dark forces.

You Are Omniscient

It may be difficult to accept that you are omniscient, but you are. However, you have been trained to believe that you are the rational mind, and there is also a modern tendency to worship reason and logic—which are helpful, yet limited tools that need to be used wisely.

The mind, in fact, has a negative bent, and most of us are victims of the psychological phenomenon called the "negativity bias." So, we tend to believe our own negative thoughts. Usually, this process causes us to ignore our wonderful intuitive insights.

But according to the yogis, our highest intelligence is based on intuition, love, compassion, and our connection with the Divine—which help us acquire the quantum mind and true divine intelligence.

I have received authentic information in dreams, or while being awake, or through streams of sensations—like calm and peaceful waves of energy that filled my body-mind. A knowingness related to an important matter would simultaneously follow—as happened with the U.S. presidential election in 2024.

In fact, I had already predicted the victory of Donald Trump in July 2024 in a Vedic astrology article that I wrote for a leading Indian magazine. The article was published in October. And one Saturday morning, I simply woke up knowing for certain the results of the election. In addition, I knew that divine beings would help America experience a very positive change.

Then, a week before the election, scheduled for November 5, I felt guided for several nights to go outside and look at the stars—each time my intuition told me that massively positive changes for the world were coming, too.

In the night sky—right on top of my bedroom window almost above my head—I saw Jupiter, the Vedic planet of higher wisdom and space. It appeared even brighter than Venus, and at times I could see the Moon. The whole sky appeared to radiate wisdom, love, optimism, and righteousness.

Another great omen was that I could see, a bit faded and distant, the Pleiades star cluster—a constellation associated with benevolent ETs with whom I feel a profound connection.

These omens meant that everything would go well for me and the world—and that we were receiving help from benevolent, higher beings who would contribute to our liberation from suffering and enslavement.

This information also spoke of the liberation of humanity from very exploitative and tyrannical individuals, who had long hoarded our resources, kept us in bondage with fear, disease and poverty, and created endless wars and famine on the Earth plane.

So, this is one of the ways I receive information about the near or distant future or about the past—including my past lives.

You, too, could suddenly receive images of a past life—for example, from a different time period with people you have met in this life. It has happened to me several times, and historical references have always proved my recollections to be accurate. Some people can even realize that they once lived on a different planet. I once had a vision that suggested this.

The yogis teach that putting your attention and meditating on some main areas of your brain can make you omniscient, and you can tap into space knowledge coming from the ether element. These psychic areas of the brain are: the midbrain, the pineal gland, and the cerebellum.

So, we are all omniscient, and we can acquire the quantum mind with both meditation and an attitude of openness. Then we will be at one with all Creation and the Goddesses—who are very benevolent, evolved, and loving. This special connection will lead you to evolution, and eventually, you will know everything. This is your destiny in this life or in a future life.

Try This

- Cultivate your intuition with acceptance, love and respect for yourself.
- Practice meditation, which is paramount for accurate predictions and connecting with a higher being like a Goddess.
- Also care for your body with love and respect—and then your intuition will blossom.
- Notice a "gut feeling" or another sensation in the body, which could be bringing you intuitive insights. Your entire body is filled with neurons—which are like mini brains—found in especially high concentrations in the belly and the brain.

Additional Intuitive Insights

A few weeks ago, as I was writing about Vesta, I was flooded with more unexpected images of the same girl whom I saw in a vision during my yoga class, many years ago. I was certain, beyond all doubt, that this young woman with chestnut hair was me during that past life in ancient Rome.

She was a pretty girl with white, pale skin, about 18 years old. So, my memories of her came back 20 years after my earlier experience on the yoga mat, when I first remembered that I had lived a life as a Vestal.

This time, it seemed strange that this girl and I were not much alike, and I felt detached as I learned more about her. And yet I knew she was me. Without even trying, I was taken back to the day when she awaited her destiny—and a possible execution.

I saw her dress—my dress—with crystal clear vision. It was a long white tunic fastened under the chest with a white cord and a knot. Missing were the veil and jewelry, and I knew intuitively that after the trial someone in court had removed my distinctive Vestal veil and my other belongings, but I could not remember the person who stripped me of my rank.

As I have written earlier, my hair was braided, a dark shade of chestnut with reddish highlights. Some wavy bangs had become loose around my face, revealing my turbulent emotional state. However, I still hoped to be absolved.

LALITHA DONATELLA RIBACK

A few days ago, I read "A Place at the Altar" by Princeton University scholar *Meghan J. DiLuzio*, and her historically based descriptions of the Vestals' lifestyle. The book explained the important role of the Vestal priestesses in Roman society and other customs.

This all rang so true that I cried bitter tears of recognition. This time as I thought about the Roman girl, I suddenly felt compassion for her, so much for my detached observations. I was instead catapulted back into that life and felt deep sorrow.

I now believe that the main reason we forget our past lives is that our minds would be flooded with such sadness, exceeding joy, or other intense emotions, and our current lives would seem irrelevant by comparison.

Then as I continued reading DiLuzio's description of the Vestals' traditional attire, I instantly realized that the vision of myself in a Vestal dress was accurate. Here is what this expert of Roman customs and history wrote:

Several statues wear their tunicae [tunics] belted beneath the breast with a Hercules knot, perhaps in order to signify their virginity.

Her description matched exactly my earlier vision of me as a Vestal girl, wearing a white tunic tied under my chest with a strange knot that I could not describe.

Then, I began thinking about the cruel Roman tradition of selecting Vestals among female children between the ages of five and ten. Immediately, I felt the trauma of so many little girls whose childhood was ended abruptly by overly ambitious parents who pushed their daughters into irrevocable priesthood.

Then, the girls would live in the House of the Vestals for 30 years, their hair would grow long and be styled in the traditional braids. Also, they would wear white virginal dresses and dedicate their lives to serving the Goddess, the Empire, and the population of Rome.

So, the Vestals' high status in society was not meant for their enjoyment, but rather, it highlighted the importance of spiritual life in Rome. In addition, the Vestals' virginity and pure lifestyle stood as forms of protection for the entire Empire. Sadly, the Vestals' lives did not belong to them—and their privilege and wealth could never make up for such lack of freedom.

For me, the only comforting aspect of that life in ancient Rome was a deep spiritual connection with Goddess Vesta—as in my heart I considered her my real mother.

An Unusual Phenomenon

Just a few days ago once more, I wondered whether my recent memories as a Vestal were accurate. So, I asked the Divine Feminine and Goddess Vesta for guidance. Before I went to sleep, I thought with strong emotion:

LALITHA DONATELLA RIBACK

Please tell me, is all this from my imagination or from my memory?

Then, that same night, I woke up for no apparent reason. I sat on the bed, and feeling thirsty, I picked up the glass of water from my nightstand. Suddenly, from the middle of my bedroom, a very loud feminine voice spoke with authority, uttering a single word:

"Memory."

This was a melodious yet strong voice with a strangely metallic or static timbre. I was scared. I thought:

Who was that?

I remained frozen, motionless. Then with my eyes I scanned the room in the semi-darkness. Soft moon rays entered from the two windows filling my bedroom with a silvery glow. I could see that I was alone. But I still decided to turn on the lamp. All seemed well.

Soon after, I fell into a deep, dreamless sleep. In the morning, as I opened my eyes, in a flash of lightening clarity, I remembered— I had asked the Goddess for a clear answer about the source of my visions. It was my *"memory,"* she said. For me this was sufficient confirmation that my spontaneous visions originated from events deeply embedded in my soul.

So, I had been a priestess who used fire rituals to connect with the Goddess. It is then no surprise that in this life, too, many years after that first vision, my spiritual teacher empowered me to perform fire rituals to invoke Vedic Goddesses, along with other celestial beings.

Also, I recently learned that the metallic, echoing quality of that female voice, was due to a difference in frequencies, as beings in higher dimensions vibrate faster than we do in our third dimension. So, the voice of a space being, who reaches out to you in a lower dimension, can sound metallic and somewhat distorted, like the echo of a voice on a mountain.

The Circular Nature of Time

Recently I woke up during the night and before I could open my eyes, two back-to-back visions appeared in a flash. Immediately, I knew that these images showed me as that same Vestal priestess, but at two different ages.

The first vision was a girl, a teenager. I could see her whole body from head to foot as she slowly walked alone at nighttime in the garden of the Atrium Vestae. I recognized myself and knew that she was returning to the House of the Vestals from an encounter with her beloved.

This time, too, she wore a white tunic, but her long wavy hair hung naturally around her shoulders and below the chest. Despite the immaculate dress, she appeared somewhat disheveled, her face flushed red, with pouty pink lips. This remote perception revealed a new sensuality that embarrassed me. In fact, this same girl had looked much more delicate and virginal in my earlier visions.

Apparently, she was fully human—and this was a surprise to me due to my idealized conception of a priestess. A hint of a smile on her full lips, a light in her dreamy eyes—she looked unmistakably like a teenager in love.

Nevertheless, she appeared innocent and completely oblivious to the grave risk of exposure. She embodied the unconscious carelessness so common among passionate youths—her thoughts fully centered on reckless love and abandon.

Intuitively, I sensed the horrified reactions of the elder Vestals at her return to the House of the Vestals. Despite their motherly support and protection, their faces revealed sheer terror as for an impending doom.

All this awareness was simply downloaded on my mind in a very short amount of time, like a *nano second*—that is one billionth of a second. Or was it rather a *femto second*—one quadrillionth of a second?

With this modern understanding of time, we can better grasp phenomena like non-local awareness, remote viewing, and spontaneous past life memories.

In the second vision immediately following the first, I saw myself again, but many years older. This time I appeared about 55 years old, my face ghostly pale, the hair still demurely braided in the

Vestal style, streaked with silver grey. My eyes displayed a severe expression of painfully acquired maturity.

In this psychic sight, it became clear that after the accusation of breaking my virginity vow, my life had been spared. Either way I had not lost my virginity. More revelations came later. Both my boyfriend and I had narrowly escaped capital punishment through sheer luck and thanks to my parents' intervention.

The emperor had pardoned my beloved, but he was demoted. I remained in the same order to serve Goddess Vesta for the rest of my life and chose not to marry after the prescribed 30 years as a priestess. Additionally, I appeared ill—and I intuitively understood that this woman was at the end of her life.

At the soul level, so much was revealed within one second—or less—just before I opened my eyes, probably because this information needed to make its way into this book. How extraordinary it was that flashes of insight brought volumes of information from my higher self.

At the physiological level, the piezoelectric qualities of the pineal gland—or third eye—and its crystalline composition allow this gland to produce higher states of consciousness, vivid images, and information from non-local sources. This phenomenon is even more frequent in that transitional state between sleep and waking up.

You can even learn about your past lives from the akashic records—or data stored in the ether, containing everything that has ever happened on Earth, in our galaxy, and in other galaxies.

These spontaneous memories can arise in your awareness to bring you deep healing or needed guidance. And the pineal gland brings you expanded consciousness from your Source, higher cosmic beings, and your own Higher Self.

My experience reveals that our conception of time is incorrect because linear time, as we perceive it in our waking state, does not exist. Instead, we are multidimensional beings living in the past, present and future simultaneously.

Moreover, we live in a simulated world, a multiverse made of vibrational sounds. And we often incarnate into a physical body to experience the same lessons over and over—until we stop wanting to reincarnate here.

Every event, the creation of a galaxy, the birth of a child, our ancient history, all happen simultaneously—and if you could time-travel, you would realize that you can go back and forth in time at any moment. You would also notice that one year of Earth-time equals a much shorter time in the higher dimensions, and in more evolved worlds.

Vesta, too, still lives and exists in both our tridimensional plane and in the higher realms of consciousness.

She lives inside you, and you can connect with her. She is everywhere. In fact, you are Vesta. She enters the hearth of every home, turning a simple building into a life center filled with energy, harmony and nourishment. She does so with the utmost positivity and pure love.

GOLDEN AGE GODDESSES

A few weeks ago, I bought a small statue of her, a handmade alabaster beauty that joined the other statues of female deities on my altar. Together, these Goddesses bring me a daily reminder of the presence of the Divine Feminine in me, as well as in every woman, man, child, and plant.

Prophecies and a New Discovery

On a cold, windy afternoon in November 2024, while chanting a mantra to Shakti—the essence of the universal Mother Goddess—I suddenly had a vision of the sky above the ancient Roman Forum.

From this aerial view of the ancient grounds, I searched for the temple of Vesta and soon spotted it—a white-marble, round building surrounded by many white Corinthian columns. I moved closer to the temple and clearly saw its shining domed roof. Soon, as I focused on the oculus, the round bronze opening at the top, smokey circles from the Goddess' flame billowed upwards—reached high above the temple and made a sacred connection between earth and the heavens.

As I viewed the puffing smoke rings moving higher into the sky, they briefly danced in the air and then slowly dispersed. Soon new smoke rings came out and again vanished in the air current. Although their smokey patterns appeared to be similar, in reality, their shapes changed each time. I then had a flashing revelation—the spiraling rings resembled those you would see in a movie with Native American Indians.

In Indian camps, in fact, men stood by a bonfire, sending smoke signals and conveying secret messages and vital information to their own people. At times, this communication was meant for nearby tribes—but in both cases, the messages were hidden in the smoke patterns.

So, could it be that the Vestals, too, were communicating secret omens arising from the Goddess' flame? After all, the priestesses could prophesize, and smokey codes exiting from the sanctum of the Goddess were probably meant for the emperor.

Also, my intuition said that other priests, from the Temple of Mars and Temple of Jupiter on the Capitoline Hill, would receive the smoke messages from the dome of the Temple of Vesta, and communicated them to the emperor.

After all, these temples were at a distance of approximately 1640 feet from the Temple of Vesta. And in good weather, smoke signals can be seen from even farther away.

From a short meditation, I learned that the Vestals told their prophecies about the future of the Roman Empire and its people through various sacrifices, and also through the fire and smoke. I suppose that the Roman high authorities would not want to divulge these prophecies and kept them secret. Most likely, this is the reason we have never heard about them.

It is interesting also, that in addition to various sacred objects of great value, the Vestals were custodians of official documents containing state secrets.

I deduced from my vision of the Temple of Vesta that the shape and color of the smoke in ceremonies added meaning to the omens. So, to prophesize, the Vestal priestesses might have used smoke along with their other divination methods.

I then remembered a tradition at the Vatican City—where the staff communicated the arrival of a new pope through a signaling method, using colored smoke from the chimney of the Sistine Chapel. Black smoke signified that the new pope had not yet been elected. Instead, white smoke meant that the College of Cardinals had elected a new pope.

Earth Goddesses

For many thousands of years, the Siddhas—the yogis with supernormal powers who existed during the time of Mu, or Lemurian civilization—lived in the Himalayas, and moved to the region of Tamil Nadu in South of India, about 50,000 years ago. These yogis always held sacred the notion that Goddesses are present in everything and everyone.

Today's Tamil Siddhas still live in meditative seclusion and are powerful healers. They can see a Goddess in every herb, plant, lake, or river. They also communicate with the Goddesses in medicinal herbs and ask them to potentiate the healing powers of their herbal preparations—to completely eradicate diseases.

And the Native Americans, too, believe in various Goddess archetypes, such as *Mother Earth*, *Changing Woman*, protecting women in all the different stages of their lives, and the luminous *White Shell Woman*, who symbolizes creation and abundance.

The Fall of Rome and Healing Plants

From my spiritual studies, meditative experiences and visions, I know that Vesta still exists as a light being both in space and in our collective unconscious. But in ancient times, her images and temples did not resist the assault of a Christian emperor.

It all started in 391 AD, when the Roman Emperor Theodosius ordered his militia to destroy all Vesta's effigies along with her main temple in the Forum. After embracing Christian beliefs, he became obsessed with eliminating the religion of Vesta. And sadly after 1,100 years, Vesta's sacred flame was permanently extinguished in 394 AD.

Just 82 years later in 476 AD, the Roman Empire fell—after 503 years of uncontested rule over a staggering 36 countries and regions in Europe, North Africa, Middle East, Asia Minor, and more.

But all together, the Roman civilization lasted 1,229 years. So, is it possible that renouncing the blessings of Vesta, the number one protector of Rome—the "first" according to Ovid—resulted in the decline of Rome's good fortunes?

According to the ancient people who considered Vesta's rites Rome's primary shield from enemies, disease, poverty, and failure, the answer is a definite—yes. And I agree. For example, when hurricane Sandy hit New York in 2012, I began chanting protective mantras—and my house was the only one on my street that did not lose the electricity in a community with over 300,000 homes. In addition, my house and garden were not damaged by the torrential rains and high winds—whereas the entire town and countless trees were devasted.

So, can you imagine the protective powers of daily group prayers over a period of 1,000 years? It is unimaginable.

When the worship of ancient Goddesses was gradually banned everywhere, those who prayed to them were also persecuted.

Also, the Temple of Vesta—with its magnificent white-marble round building, columns and life-size statues—was dismantled. Regrettably, in the following centuries, all its materials were stolen and used to build palaces for popes and various royals.

However, in an unfair twist of fate, other temples dedicated to male Gods experienced a better destiny. For example, in the Forum Boarium in Rome, a 2nd century BC temple dedicated to the male deity Hercules Victor remains well preserved even today. The temple was also restored countless times throughout the centuries and is now surrounded by a stern, black iron fence to keep the population away.

Even when the Temple of Hercules was damaged in the 1st century AD, ten of its original columns were replaced with new ones made of Carrara marble. Then the temple became a church in the year 1132, and the temple's original dignity was preserved. Was this a coincidence? Probably not.

In fact, history says that during the Inquisition, over 300,000 women were burned alive for simply praying to a Goddess or using healing herbs. But I believe that the real number of deaths was actually much higher.

So, both women and Goddesses underwent the same persecution. Vesta, too, was a healer, and in ancient Rome women would flock to her temple to pray for their loved ones, as I learned from Amedeo Lanciani's book about his archeological finds.

In addition, ancient Romans offered plants and special foods to Vesta to connect with her and receive her blessings. She was the protectress of femininity, and especially loved the chasteberry tree, the *vitex agnus-castus*, whose white flowers emitted a pungent but pleasant scent. Just like in ancient Rome, the seeds of chasteberry are still used today as a healing treatment for women's reproductive system.

Also, like in the Vedic tradition, in ancient Rome, flowers held a central place in all the ceremonies to Vesta. So, the Romans understood the power of flowers to purify the body-mind, and used their petals in special medicinal and sacred preparations.

From ancient records, we also know that the Vestal Virgins burned frankincense, myrrh as incense, and oak twigs to enliven the embers and feed the fire on the altar of Vesta.

Today, too, we burn frankincense and myrrh in religious ceremonies and use flowers' essential oils as aromatherapy to reach higher levels of relaxation.

Even scientists say that smelling flowers leads to the activation of the limbic system and the production of *serotonin, oxytocin, endorphins and dopamine*, the feel-good hormones. I know that as a Vestal, I offered the Goddess flower petals and garlands and also honored her by burning olive oil lamps.

In addition, the Vestals placed as special offerings in the fire ritual small pieces of *mola salsa*—the *focaccia* bread made from salty spelt flour. The preparation of mola salsa also required that the dough be mixed with holy water from the *Egeria* sacred spring. Egeria, in fact, was highly revered as a water Goddess of extreme beauty and believed to live in this spring along with other nymphs. And it was customary to add fresh wine, oil, and milk to the fire. Also, the *Vestales Maximae* or elder Vestals prepared beautifully braided breads and distributed them among the devotees attending the rituals.

Despite their disciplined and demanding ritual schedule, the Vestal priestesses enjoyed special luxuries and privileges. Dressed in white, head covered by a demure veil, they inspired deep awe among the population, as they traveled in the city on their own carriages accompanied by lictor guards, who protected them at all times. Moreover, the Vestals attended the most exclusive cultural and spiritual events in Rome. These special dispensations were rare even among the royals and nobility.

Yet as women, the Vestals did not even exist and rarely married after age 40. More often than not, they chose to live isolated in the House of the Vestals and serve the Goddess for the rest of their lives.

Goddesses of Fire and Water

Titus Livius wrote:

"There was a forest irrigated in the middle by a perennial source of water that flowed from a shady cave. Numa Pompilius often went there without witnesses to meet with the Goddess…Egeria, his wife". (Livy – History of Rome)

So, Livy wrote that the second king of Rome, Numa Pompilius, was married to a river Goddess, Egeria. Numa, in fact, hailed from a matriarchal society in the Sabina region, northeast of Rome in central Italy—in which people followed Goddess religions.

Like the ancient yogis, the Romans believed that Goddesses and nymphs lived in springs, rivers, and lakes. These bodies of water included natural founts and were considered deeply sacred as they embodied the Divine Feminine.

In my childhood, I loved drawing nymphs dancing under the full moon near fountains, wells, and lakes. I also felt a deep connection with the Moon, and the demi-goddesses known as nymphs. So, neither Barbie nor Disney were my primary attractions, and my devotion went to Angels, Jesus, Mother Mary, and the sacred feminine found in ancient myths.

We have ample evidence that human consciousness dropped for over 5,000 years during Kali Yuga—the cycle of great injustice, widespread destruction, human enslavement, and suppression of the Divine Feminine—that we have just left.

During that time, foundational knowledge about the four major Earth cycles called Yugas—and their effects on both human consciousness and world events—were forgotten.

Fortunately, the Kali Yuga ended in 2023, according to the Tamil Siddha yogis of India.

But Vesta's shining form and deep love will remain forever pure, because she is the embodiment of compassion for all beings, especially women.

And I believe that Vesta is here on Earth—not as a formal religion, which could make her a mere institution devoid of substance—but as a superconsciousness that brings love and protection for humanity. In fact, her nurturing qualities will be of great assistance in this transitional time into the Golden Age, when we need to heal both the Earth and ourselves.

Also, remember that you are Vesta—and as mind boggling and this sounds—you are one and the same with the Divine.

I consider my dreams, visions and memories of a past life as a worshipper of Vesta as testimony to the return of the Goddess. Another sign is that I recently discovered a contemporary Roman organization that celebrates Vesta's rites of water purification and the burning flame. Its female members even dress up as Vestals in beautiful and historically accurate fashion.

I know that my recent one-pointed attention on Vesta, as well as my research, have brought her back into my life. In fact, last night as the Moon entered its full-moon phase, I had several dreams about Vesta. She carried a powerful and loving energy. In one dream, I was instructed to first pray to my Ancestors, and then, in an emphatic and regal tone, I was told to invoke, "Her, the One who is." I felt I was receiving an empowerment, and was initiated again into her sacred rites. "I am that I am," says a Biblical phrase. Yes, I am.

But sometimes, I feel pain for both the suppression of the Divine Feminine and the disappearance of priestesses. I also feel the rebellion and devastation of those innocent Vestals found guilty of breaking their chastity vow, which led to a cruel death by being buried alive.

And what to say of some wicked Roman leaders? Emperor Domitian alone, during his brief 16-year reign, became hell-bent on destroying the Roman elites and the Vestals. As a result, he accused four Vestal virgins of breaking their vow and had them buried alive.

I believe that this blood-thirsty emperor chose to execute those young women mostly due to his own misogyny than his adherence to Roman law. Historical records, in fact, show that some Vestals were condemned and killed even for dressing "too elegantly," a behavior considered a sure sign of *incestum*—the Latin term for breaking the virginity vow.

History Uncovered: The Destruction of Ancient Rome

Following an unstoppable attack against Goddess religions that began in the 4th century AD, Vesta's temple underwent a total demolition in 1549. We have seen that the temple's beautiful materials and exquisite white marble slabs and tiles were stolen to be used to build palaces for popes.

In 1877, the great archeologist Rodolfo Amedeo Lanciani discovered the remains of the Temple of Vesta and the Atrium Vestae, which he unearthed.

His archeological finds included 11 life-size statues of Vestals, pedestals, and the remains of many more statues mostly depicting famous *Vestales Maximae* or high priestesses.

Lanciani lamented the "irreparable loss to culture and progress" following the recycling of ancient marbles, and the sad fate of ancient Roman sites, especially religious ones—like the sudden disappearance of the last remains of the temple of Jupiter Optimus Maximus, and thousands of pounds of gold.

Ancient Roman coins showed Vesta's round temple, its conical roof and the oculus that let out the smoke produced by the sacred flame. This round construction was completed with a sacred central hearth hosting the eternal flame and was surrounded by twenty Corinthian columns built on a podium fifteen meters in diameter.

But some coins focused on the power of Vesta, showing her as she sat in the center of the temple holding a libation bowl that indicated nurturing and abundance, and a scepter—the symbol of her supremacy.

Many invasions by barbaric populations, like the Goths and the Vandals, in addition to the Saracens, the French, and even Napoleon devastated Rome with sacking and bloody battles. So it is a miracle that we still have a Roman Forum, and that there are remains of the Goddess temple—however, the biggest structures remaining are due to a reconstruction project that began in the 1930s.

Vestal Priestesses

The Vestal virgins held considerable political power. A slave or other person accused of a crime would be instantly forgiven if he or she happened to come across a Vestal—a sign that the Divine wanted the accused to receive mercy and salvation.

Also, the Vestals were the only women in Rome who could testify in court without an oath—because their words were considered always sacred and therefore true.

Moreover, the six Vestals lived in elegant surroundings, aided by many slaves and servants who cleaned after the ceremonies and maintained the House of the Vestals' grounds and its beautiful gardens.

Deeply revered for their piety and purity, these priestesses were shown deference in the streets, where pedestrians gave way to their *lecticas*, a luxurious palanquin covered with silk drapes. People respectfully stepped aside at their passage—both to give honor and due to a legal requirement, reserved also for the emperor and high officials.

However, sincere love for the Vestals ran deep in the hearts of the Roman people, who shared a widespread belief that their happiness and well-being and the continuity of the Empire depended on the priestesses' performance of solemn ceremonies to Vesta.

A Mysterious Goddess

Today, my heart longs for Vesta, and we can barely find any images of her beauty and perfection. In fact, at the time when her religion was uprooted, the idea of "paganism" landed on our planet, and we became afraid of connecting with celestial beings other than those approved by religious and political authorities.

When I was a child, paganism was a foreign concept for me, and I still disregard that idea today, as I consider it a form of prejudice. In the Vedic tradition there has always been more respect for all celestial beings, sages, and holy people in general. In the Rig Veda we find many mentions of the *Apsaras*, the divine nymphs, celestial dancers and singers connected to water.

Fortunately, we are leaving behind the era of great ignorance—the Kali Yuga—in which some leaders of organized religions had taken control of our consciousness, managing the way we relate to the Divine and calling "idolatry" any interaction with images of other faiths. I believe this was a great misconception.

In fact, the much more ancient Vedas mention millions of Gods and Goddesses, and in rituals brahmins use imagery of cosmic beings—which makes them more relatable, and easier to contact through invocation and powerful vibrational sounds called *mantras*. A personal relationship is key to connect with a Goddess and experience miracles.

The term "pagan" denies the existence of fairies, nymphs, and millions—if not billions—of higher cosmic beings existing in different galaxies, dimension and frequencies.

And while we do not need to worship these beings, we can engage in an open communication with them and use their images as an inspirational tool.

Also, I believe that the term "paganism" will become obsolete as we humans will expand our cosmology, and a higher understanding of the Divine will dawn on Earth during the Golden Age.

We are in a transitional time of healing and understanding the evils that were unleashed against humanity—when we were suppressed, tortured, and lied to for thousands of years. And the wealth and Earth's resources were in the hands of a few people, who hoarded everything valuable and enslaved human beings.

The violent removal of early religions and the concealment of our human history were used to dumb down our consciousness, since each new leader, both secular and spiritual, aggressively pushed new gods, cults, policies, customs, and currencies. I believe that all this happened to the detriment of our intelligence and freedom.

Humanity is now rebelling and refusing to accept any lies, unlawful impositions, and unfair limitations—and this is allowing the Divine Feminine of miracles, love and compassion to take over our predicaments and bring us solutions. Family values are back. Freedom is back. Truth is back.

Again, what once was called "worship" is simply a way to communicate with a benevolent being, a friend, who is invisible to our eyes and who lives in a higher density. We are not inferior, we are simply vibrating differently and depending on our limited senses. Soon, our psychic abilities will become more powerful and will give us access to a more accurate cosmology.

In their mad run for supremacy, political leaders had banned and ridiculed the worship of, or communication with many Goddesses—calling it superstition, legend, and sin.

And devotees, left with no other choice, began worshipping the Goddess in secret, practicing with other adepts in underground caves. But too often, devotees feared for their lives and abandoned their religion altogether.

The Goddess Protects Life

The Golden Age is the time of the righteous, benevolent Goddesses. If you have a tendency to cave in and let others decide for you in important matters, Vesta will give you sovereignty and authority.

She also gives you:

- Authority to restore peace in your home after an argument or bad news.
- Authority to trust yourself and make your home a sacred, safe haven.
- Authority to support your family both emotionally and physically.
- Authority to heal yourself and others.

So, the Goddess can give you power. Fortunately, in the Golden Age, we will be able to activate our divine DNA. This is already happening on Earth, and we are undergoing a huge shift in consciousness thanks to higher frequencies and more light coming from both the Sun and our galaxy. Earth, too, is evolving—and Mother Earth needs our spirit of love, collaboration, and forgiveness.

We will be able to relate to each other with less judgment and more authenticity, based on greater love and caring. Relationships will soon heal—and children will be brought up with love by two empowered, loving beings—not two traumatized humans who did their best to contain their negative thoughts.

The Goddess will bring spiritual solutions changing the hearts of men, supporting women and children and turning this planet into a Heaven on Earth.

We should never again undergo the shocking events of the past, like what recently happened on the New York City subway, when a man set a woman on fire—then watched her die. Two other men and a male policeman witnessed this horrific crime, but none intervened to help the poor woman. Chilling videos of their apparent indifference, as they filmed the whole tragedy on their phones, seemed even more bloodcurdling than the murder.

Only the Goddess can save us when men become disconnected from their humanness. When instead of protecting life, they grow cold and indifferent to the loss of life and loss of children who are kidnapped and trafficked, raped and killed—the world is finished. So, to jumpstart the Creation and return to our sacredness, we need to bring back love and safety for all—and this is what the Goddess does best because, like a mother, she cares.

Myth

Kali is an aspect of a Hindu Goddess who became extremely fierce, ferocious, and set out to destroy the world, when she became horrified because humans were committing all kinds of sins—and causing incredible pain to each other.

Using her invincible shakti, she chased evil people, beheaded them and wore their skulls tied as a bloody garland around her neck. And so she continued on a rampage, killing criminals, destroying entire cities with utmost rage and might. Having lost all control, her tongue began sticking out of her mouth, and her very long hair fell unkempt on her naked body.

Shiva, her consort became very worried that she would destroy the entire Creation and, knowing his wife well, he appealed to her love and compassion—as he laid on the ground pretending to be dead.

The sight of her dead beloved stopped the Goddess in her tracks—and kneeling next to her husband's seemingly lifeless body, she was flooded with so much love for him that her rage vanished. Together, Shiva and Kali walked away from all the destruction and horrors and began rebuilding the world when Shiva followed his wife into her dance of creation.

So, love is the solution to fix all distortions to our originally divine and loving makeup—because we cannot simultaneously feel love and hatred.

The Goddess is love and she is standing behind women. And women are upset—and want to save the children from wars and murderers, even more so than they care to save themselves.

Of course, some women, too, are involved in child sex trafficking and other crimes against humanity, but the violence against life in the past 5,000 years of Kali Yuga started with men, as women were more inclined to choose love, life, compassion and relationships. Some men may have had a different experience, but for millennia, heartlessness has reigned on Earth.

When man-made law could not protect women—only a divine solution could right wrongs. The return of divine protection and true love, the return of repentance, the return of truth will heal everyone's trauma—and especially the horrific crimes against women and children. The love of the Divine Mother will heal everyone, men and women after human laws have failed to protect us.

The Goddess archetype will also heal widespread trauma, bringing back righteousness, so that we humans will be able to work together to ensure that women will be respected and protected, empowered and given their rightful place on our new Earth.

Men, too, will be empowered with their newly activated divine masculinity—a protective, courageous and compassionate masculinity strengthened by righteousness, and men will be afforded the same love, respect, and protection.

The Light Has Returned

Light is intelligence. And we are witnessing the arrival of larger quantities of light from the Sun, bringing higher consciousness and divine frequencies—so we are now free to recreate ourselves. Soon we will learn that we are loved, we are powerful beyond belief, and both sovereign and divine. Astronomers, too, are telling us that the Sun has changed. There are so many solar storms at this time, big waves of solar activity, extraordinary solar flares, and a massive push of energy.

The higher galactic beings have returned—they are the "Gods" and "Goddesses" of antiquity. They are actually us in the future, and we are them. So, we are interconnected by the law of *dharma* or righteousness, and loving duty. We are one and we are waking up from a long sleep, needing much healing.

Rome's Grandiose Spirituality

The Eternal City of Rome has had a deeply spiritual past—which might go unnoticed by those who only explore its imperial history and contemporary amenities.

For example, Lanciani, the expert Italian archeologist, found 4th century guide books of Rome that listed a staggering 424 temples, 304 shrines, and a vast population of statues of Gods.

There were over 80 life-size statues made of precious metals, 64 made of ivory, 3785 statues made of bronze, and the marble statues were too numerous to count.

In sum, it was said that Rome possessed such a high number of divine statues to equal the number of its living 700,000 inhabitants.

For me, Vesta still embodies the joy and love that are inherent in women and the hearth and the sacred fire found in each home, alchemically transmuting feelings and foods into love and turning them into energy for our physical, emotional, and spiritual lives.

I am deeply saddened by the banning of her worship, but again, as Joseph Campbell said, *"You cannot kill a God"* nor a Goddess.

Myth

Vesta's extraordinary beauty and purity attracted the attention of Neptune and Apollo, who became erotically attracted to her and tried to seduce her while she slept.

But a braying donkey awakened Vesta, saving her from the assault. Miraculously, the Goddess was able to flee and went into hiding to preserve her purity, sovereignty, and freedom.

Then the donkey remained Vesta's favorite animal—occasionally appearing with her in paintings and bas reliefs. In addition, during the Vestalia festivals, donkeys were garlanded with both flowers and baked bread as a tribute to the Goddess.

Our Worst Enemy

I believe that the donkey symbolized simplicity devoid of any ego. In fact, in the Vedic wisdom tradition, the ego is considered the ultimate obstacle to spiritual enlightenment.

Ego can lead to self-destruction through:
- Separation from God and others
- Lack of love
- Contempt for ourselves and others
- Hatred

- Forgetting that we are One
- Jealousy or comparison with others
- Greed, dissatisfaction, and lack of joy
- Limitations blocking infinite possibilities
- Ignorance of our divine nature and power
- Fear of the unknown
- Low self-esteem
- Dependence on the senses
- Pride

And the list goes on and on...

Infinite Feminine Power

Vesta's nature as pure fire ignited life itself. She guarded women's well-being through purification from dark forces, and supported women's safety and chastity, the happiness within the home, and was the center of all life in Rome. Also, Vesta was associated with the ultimate feminine power—and was preeminent.

Yesterday, I offered Vesta an earthen lamp of olive oil with a few drops of wine and milk. I placed fresh flowers next to her white alabaster statue. Then I chanted a mantra invoking her name and blessings and replenished and burned the lamp until I went to sleep at night.

In ancient times, Vesta's fire was refreshed and started anew only once a year. So I feel that restarting Vesta's sacred fire once a day is very appropriate for our accelerating time of ascension to the 5th dimension—as in the Golden Age of the Goddess, time passes faster.

Also, I now look forward to my next trip to Rome, where I will visit her temple and sacred grounds for the first time in this life. I look forward to taking my steps on the ancient cobblestone—the *lapis tiburtinus* in the Forum. Lovingly, like a pilgrim, I will make my way through the dusty terrain to the temple.

Today, Valli, a human Goddess and fully empowered priestess, helped me pray to Vesta through a magnificent fire ritual. We invoked Vesta in the fire fed by pure ghee—a byproduct of cow milk. In the Vedic culture, cow milk is considered very pure and sacred.

In today's fire prayer, we asked Vesta to increase and restore harmony and nurturing in our homes. We asked for beautiful homes for all—living spaces filled with infinite love, abundant nourishment, and total protection. We also prayed for the safety of women everywhere.

The blessed, purifying flame of the ritual symbolized a luminous union between Vedic and ancient Roman rites, all in the holy name of the Divine Feminine. As the fire rose higher, I felt the blessings of the Mother Protectress, the Creatress of all the galaxies—and Queen of the multiverse.

As the firelight grew towards the ceiling, my body responded to the sacred mantras with a tingling sensation that filled my mind with awe and bliss. We invoked the name of the Goddess multiple times—each generating higher and higher frequencies. I knew that sincerely invoking Vesta further activated her pure presence in me.

The Vestals' Special Aura

Since their early childhood, the pure priestesses of Vesta lived like Goddesses on Earth during a dark time for humanity. Not only did they receive extensive education into the secret rites of the Feminine Divine, but they also spent their lives in deep connection with the Goddess, participating day and night in all her rituals and, often, in other spiritual activities in Rome.

They selflessly ensured that the flame in the sanctum remained alive at all times, even during long sleepless nights—and stood out for their uniquely feminine beauty, steadfastness, and godly qualities.

Celibacy per se does not qualify as a divine quality—and in the Vedas, the Goddesses protect both creation and sexuality.

But of course, celibacy can help transcend the senses for those who deliberately choose such a mystical path. However, celibacy as a requirement for the Vestals seems an attempt at controlling their shakti and feminine energy. This suppression of the feminine, in fact, has pervaded the last 5,000 years of Kali Yuga.

The Godly Woman

The following qualities were inspired by "Habits of a Godly Woman" by author Joyce Mayer, who beautifully praised the habits and characteristics of godly women, or as I call them, Goddess women.

Usually, these women display:
- Forgiveness
- Simplicity
- Effortless beauty
- Trust in God
- Faith
- Hope
- Positive thinking
- Service to others
- Excellence in all they do
- Self-discipline
- Nurturing
- Healing

Can men also embrace these same habits? Absolutely.

The Vestals tended the eternal flame, and they, too, were Godly women—embodying the best of the Roman ideal and venerated for both their knowledge and sacred rituals.

However, their sexuality did not belong to them, and despite their divine service to the Goddess and state, they could die if found guilty of breaking the virginity vows. They lived, otherwise, a life of influence, inspiring love and awe among the fascinated people of Rome.

The Goddess never wanted her Vestal priestesses to be dehumanized. The way Jesus never asked his apostles to be celibate. Jesus went to weddings and provided fresh wine for all, to ensure everyone would have a good time and honored and celebrated the newly married couple.

The more beautiful Vestals probably faced higher risks of losing their lives as they exerted a stronger attraction over men. Both genders, though, risked paying the ultimate price for simply being human.

Vesta's rites were tended by prophetic, divine women knowledgeable in ancient rituals, and spiritualized femininity—who wanted the happiness and health of all women and men.

These girls and women shined for both intelligence and loveliness—and were handpicked in childhood for their physical perfection and mental health, free from blemishes or defects in speech and skill. So why waste their lives through fear and death? There is no good answer for this injustice.

The Vestal Virgins' Daily Life

We have seen that Vestals embodied both the ideal Roman woman and priestess, and they were among the most educated women in Rome. Brides imitated the Vestals' braided hairstyle, and rich matrons invited them to their homes for special functions, as the affluent women wished to add an aura of sanctity even to their mundane events.

So, the priestesses of Vesta were both greatly admired for their virginal beauty and held a high status in society. Also, their most important role was keeping their physical, mental and spiritual purity—an overwhelming aim for most people during the darker age of Kali Yuga.

Physically they observed absolute cleanliness—considered vital for the performance of all rituals. Their conduct in speech, dress, and behavior needed to be impeccable, and they were required to avoid scandals and remain celibate during the 30-year service to Goddess Vesta.

They were also well versed in religious rites, literature, law, and history—at a time when many women were illiterate, they were proficient in both reading the classics and writing.

The elder Vestals, or Vestales Maximae, were in charge of keeping important records, and managing the treasury, which included funds for running the Atrium Vestae, its maintenance, and elaborate religious activities. In addition, they were involved in the overseeing the servants' work, they managed the supplies, and supervised the suitability of all living spaces.

Moreover, the Vestals had unique legal rights that set them apart from the rest of the population. These included the power to free prisoners, own property, and write wills. In addition, upon completing their service, they were granted significant honors, including a considerable pension, as well as the right to marry.

Moreover, they were the guardians of some very sacred objects that they kept in secret vaults within the temple, along with extremely important legal documents—like the will of the emperor.

All Vestals would rise early before dawn to perform their religious duties. After their bath, they tended the Sacred Fire, ensuring that the sacred flame in the Temple of Vesta never went out. They would add wood and performed the prescribed ceremonies.

During the day, they again engaged in prayers, both for the state and for private individuals, and participated in rituals at other temples, or performed special ceremonies involving chanting, fire, flowers, and other offerings—depending on the necessities and aims of the ritual.

All eyes focused on the Vestals during their public appearances. And not only were they highly respected, appearing in public during festivals, processions, and state ceremonies, but their presence was considered very auspicious, and an indication that the Gods blessed both Rome and the Empire.

The Power of Fire and Prayer

Dr. Pillai says that a fire ritual becomes the *carbonization of thought*, and carbon information-bearing atoms. Thoughts are also the most fundamental form of energy, and fire is energy. So, the pure thoughts and words of a Vestal priestess could manifest desired outcomes through sound waves and prayers. In this way, a Vestal manifested protection for all, wealth for all, food for all, and safety for all.

I truly believe that Vesta contributed to sustaining one of the most powerful empires in the ancient world. And it was the superconsciousness of the Goddess that had incredible influence on the minds and hearts of all Romans.

The suppression of a religion that brought so much love and protection clearly had a negative effect on the health, relationships, events, geology, human lifespan, frequencies, animals, nature, and consciousness everywhere in the Roman Empire.

If this seems like an exaggeration, just think of the power of one yogi to control the weather—as we have countless stories of yogis and even aborigines who can pray to bring rain and end draughts. So, clearly, spiritual technology works.

And due to the principle that everything is connected, as above so below, the physical and spiritual are also connected.

So, both in ancient times and today, the shakti power of the Goddess holds the most positive and life-supporting energy.

Finally, in the minds of all Romans, Vesta was life itself. As Ovid wrote, Vesta was *Tellus*, Earth herself. Vesta embodied the Earth Mother Goddess—sustaining life even during very dark times, when slavery, murders, wars, and bloody conquests were the norm even in the civilized and refined Roman Empire.

Thanking Vesta

It has been a great honor to talk to my beloved Goddess Vesta and share my experiences with you.

I now thank her in my own words:

I call on you, the One who is, the first Goddess of Rome and Earth. I call on you, Vesta. I invoke you in the light codes of fire and the divine language of mantras.

I call on you in the sacred and perfected Sanskrit language:

Om Vesta Deviyei Namaha

I ask you, Vesta, to grant us protection and prosperity, and activate our fiery light bodies. May your splendid form return into the consciousness of humanity, bringing us perfect nourishment, happy and safe homes, and healthy families. Thank you, thank you for returning with your empowering flame and rays of light.

Try This:

- To say the name of Vesta out loud is to bring her into your awareness. When you say her name, the higher frequency in her name's syllables will bring her before you. You become her.
- Meditate on the qualities of Goddess Vesta. Which ones do you already embody?
- Which of her qualities would you like to experience?
- Ask the Earth Goddess to grant you pure beauty, pure thoughts, great self-love, genius intelligence—the pure fire of intellect—and divine intuition and wisdom.
- Vesta can purify your beauty, so you won't depend on fashion and makeup alone to feel beautiful and highly feminine. Ask her for the capacity to manifest safety, healing, joy, and happiness.
- Men can ask Vesta to feel comfortable with their own compassion and loving feelings, keeping their heart chakra pure and free from hatred and jealousy.
- Ask Vesta to increase your self-respect and remind you of your inborn sovereignty— whether you are a man or a woman.
- Ask her to make your home a very lovely, deeply nurturing, and safe place.

- Visualize Vesta—one of the higher cosmic beings known as the Seeders, who are bringing us higher frequencies, cosmic support, love and friendship. See her as a loving mother, with a gentle voice—she does not want animal sacrifices, in fact, she abhors them.
- Vesta can be a part of your daily life—so imagine yourself as powerful, loving, safe and protected. Now, the Divine Feminine can support your life.

CHAPTER 5
DURGA MATA

The feminine is power. That's why in the Goddess tradition of India, the Goddess is called Shakti. Shakti means energy, power. -Dr. Pillai

Sitting at home on a comfortable armchair, I was meditating by listening to Dr. Pillai's voice from a recording on my computer. It was October and the first night of Navaratri that means the sacred Nine Nights of the Goddess.

"Visualize the Goddess wearing a red dress. Her hair is black, and she has a beautiful face, because she is the Goddess."

Surprised, I saw Durga behind my closed eyes as if she were in the room with me. I could see her red dress as she sat on a huge lion, whose head appeared so close to me that it looked tridimensional and very real. This was the first time that Durga visited me in a meditation. I had not tried to summon her—yet she appeared.

Traditionally it is said that praying to the Goddess in the middle of the night, avoiding sleep, can bring you both heightened awareness and supernormal powers. So I decided to stay awake the whole night, expecting to feel very tired in the morning.

But after the long meditation, I was not sleepy, and a nearly superhuman energy came over me. In the morning, despite my lack of sleep, I still felt energized, so I went running outside.

After this workout, I felt incredibly alert and strong for the entire day—and among other feats, I worked for many hours, which would have been difficult even after a good night's sleep. Then I was able to conceive the next chapter of my life and intuitively received great ideas I wanted to implement right away.

I wrote down these goals in a pretty diary, and within a few months, I achieved them one by one. Such was the power of Durga's shakti, that inundated my entire body, mind and soul.

She Comforts and Heals Your Broken Heart

Some days of our lives unfold in alternate states of pain, anger, and fear. At such times, the benevolent yet fierce presence of

Durga can remove all blockages, banish weakness in our body-mind, and grant us courage, energy, and invincibility.

Large, expressive eyes, almost terrifying despite her serene facial expression, Durga hails from the Vedic tradition as the Goddess who can kill the most powerful demons. She restores peace, truth and justice and defeats evil forces. Evil forces can cause us lethargy or lack of motivation—which can destroy opportunities and success in our lives.

Durga's primary life purpose consisted of killing Mahishasura, the most terrible demon who had acquired supernormal powers through worshipping Brahma, the creator God.

On the one hand, Durga can grant you a happy and meaningful life on Earth. It is her loving presence in all beings that ignites love in all the universes. And she is one of the forms of the Supreme Mother Goddess, Shakti.

On the other hand, the Goddess is a powerful destroyer of evil beings, who enjoy causing humanity terrible suffering. These demons tremble at the mention of her name—and they scatter away, realizing their own ultimate impotence. In fact, Durga vanquishes demons by the use of her countless super weapons, more dangerous than nuclear bombs.

Myth

The Vedic scriptures described a time when frustrated male Gods realized their inability to destroy some terrible asuras or demonic beings who were growing ever more powerful.

Realizing that the shakti of the Goddess alone had the power to eliminate all evil, they prayed for the birth of a virgin Goddess and called her Durga.

Each of the Gods offered Durga his own weapons, putting all hopes and faith in her. The Gods also witnessed Durga effortlessly defeating the arrogant demons who were enslaving and killing humans.

Unstoppable, wearing a red dress, a bejeweled gold crown on her young head, carrying her ten frightening weapons in her eight arms, a hint of a gentle smile, and a luminous, radiant complexion—she rode a huge lion whose large muscles seemed to be bursting through its skin.

The Goddess' great beauty, her serene facial expression, and her regal demeanor revealed her identity as the most powerful Goddess. Then the demons recognized Shakti—as their smirks turned to terror, followed by their quick death.

Moreover, the young Goddess began inspiring much love and devotion in righteous people—and she helped her devotees live happy, pure and noble lives.

At times, Durga rode a galloping, menacing tiger, suddenly appearing at places where demons were committing atrocities against women, children, men and Gods. Durga then battled and won against the asuras that caused death, fear, lethargy, depression, and hopelessness. She then effortlessly decapitated all demons.

I feel so blessed writing about Durga, and I believe that I was inspired by her during the days dedicated to her during October Navaratri. It is believed that Gods rejoice at the sight of Durga's immense powers to end suffering and restore justice and dharma.

The lovely, youthful Goddess displays her unstoppable power to tame even the most aggressive of egos and bring back peace.

Try This

- If you experience a lack of motivation or confusion in your financial goals or personal life, invoke Durga with her name. Ask her for help.
- Ask her to remove your lethargy.
- Request her assistance to acquire clarity, motivation and enthusiasm to recreate yourself and experience your supernormal powers. She will help you defeat negativity in yourself or in your environment.
- Take a shower, wear a red dress (if you are a man, you can wear a red handkerchief or red shirt).
- Experience your love and compassion for humanity oppressed by famine, lack of clean water, bad weather, poverty, wars, disease, and natural disasters.

- Invoke Durga, ask her to quickly intervene and help end all injustices—mostly caused by the wealthiest people on this planet, who have been hoarding all the wealth throughout millennia.
- Say out loud, "Durga, with your compassion, bring health, resources, safety, and joy among the people of Earth."
- Buy her statue online. Offer to the statue a red flower, light a candle and a stick of sweet incense. Then, place a fruit or candy in front of her.
- Always visualize what you want and the wonderful changes you want to experience on Earth.
- Ask Durga to protect you from negativity.
- Thank Durga.
- Thank and congratulate yourself for the courage to help stop evil on Earth. Even your smallest contribution to create a Heaven on Earth multiplied by billions of people can help humanity experience a Golden Age.

CHAPTER 6

MEENAKSHI, THE SUPREME GODDESS OF MADURAI

Statue worship is very powerful because when you observe it, you will see the brain responding to those images. -Dr. Pillai

With great zest, my Indian driver and the elderly guide poured rivulets of vegetable curry over their small pyramids of white rice. I liked the green banana leaves used in India as plates—both as a sound ecological choice and for their beautiful design.

The elderly guide reached out and took a chapati flatbread from a huge Thali platter, covered with lots of tiny bowls filled with appetizing foods. I looked away, as a sting in my stomach reminded me that the last food I ate was at breakfast, 7 hours earlier.

Eating at road-side restaurants held a serious health risk for a foreigner like me, with an untrained immune system. Yet it took me monumental discipline to ignore the fragrant dishes.

Hungrily, I eyed a small cup filled to the brim with homemade yogurt, and another with my favorite sambar soup made with spicy tamarind, mixed with abundant curry leaves and ground lentils.

It was a hot day in February 2019, and after a Goddess retreat with my Guru, I had stayed in India to embark on another pilgrimage to visit the temples recommended by a Nadi astrologer.

Half asleep, sitting in a small Indian car with a driver and a guide, I had been traveling since 7 a.m. through the state of Tamil Nadu. We had driven through the lush countryside on dirt roads and through crowded villages, before entering an impressively new highway. After visiting two Shiva temples, it was already late afternoon when we finally stopped at the roadside restaurant.

The worried restaurant owner seemed anxious to offer a memorable hospitality, as he kept inquiring why I was not eating. He returned several times with offerings of chai, masala dosa and rice pudding. I declined each time, to which he responded with big smiles of apology.

I knew that even a small cup of tea made with south Indian water brought the danger of water poisoning—a painful sickness I had experienced ten years earlier in Kodaikanal, and which I would not wish even on my worst enemy. I remained sick for years after. I had also read an article in the Times of India that in a nearby state, every four hours one person died from water intoxication.

I reluctantly picked at a small individual bag of Lays potato chips—a much safer yet unappetizing option. I planned to eat dinner later that night after returning to my 4-star hotel, where the staff cooked with filtered water, and made my morning chai from bottles of Aquafina.

Distractedly, I looked around the restaurant. Then suddenly everything stood still. My gaze went to a large picture on the wall—a framed print of an Indian painting. Against the plain dark background was a majestic temple with a tall, multicolored gopura.

Standing in front of the temple were three celestial looking beings—or were they extraterrestrial visitors? The two men and a woman of dignified appearance wore tall conic gold crowns splendidly carved, studded with multicolor gems.

A beautiful woman with soft-green skin appeared between the two blue-skinned men. The beings looked slim and graceful, and the sacred surroundings gave them an otherworldly appearance. I felt as though I had known them forever, only I did not remember from where. I kept observing their beautiful, realistic figures, and noticed their aristocratic bearing.

The yogis and the Tamil Siddhas with supernormal powers have written of their encounters with the Devas or "shining beings," benevolent extraterrestrials who were millions of years more evolved than us.

I began to wonder about which star system hosted beings with blue and green skin. I looked again at the woman with the delicate figure in the center of the picture. The scene seemed to have been painted exclusively for her. Her large, attractive and slanted eyes demurely cast down; she held her small hand on the palm of one of the men. The other handsome man looked benevolently upon the couple.

Moreover, the royal woman stood in the abhanga dance pose, a posture emphasizing the curves of her torso and hips, shifting the weight of her slender body to one leg. I had practiced this pose many times in my classical Odissi dance class, and I considered it an ultimately feminine and graceful pose.

Mesmerizing for her otherworldly beauty, the woman wore an alien-looking attire of low-slung, horizontally striped pants bearing her navel and a bra revealing her feminine curves.

The bare-chested men also wore horizontally striped pants covered with gold ornaments. All three ET-looking beings were barefoot, and I had the impression that they were moving slowly and gracefully. I observed the woman's small feet and toes covered with ceremonial kumkum, a holy red powder used in temples. The men's foreheads, too, were adorned with a tiny red dot between their eyebrows.

A large caption at the bottom of the painting read: Arulmiku Meenakshi Sundareswarar Thirukkalyanam, Madurai. In a flash of recognition, I remembered the city of Madurai, which I had visited many times throughout the years traveling in India. Lost in these thoughts, I forgot where I was. I noticed the picture's glass, foggy with dusty humidity. It seemed sacrilegious to neglect such beauty, and I wished that someone would bring a cloth and window cleaner to wipe the glass.

"Ma'am, we are ready to go." The driver's voice startled me, and I stood up, my head still turned to the picture. I immediately asked the guide if he knew the identity of those beings.

"It's the marriage of Goddess Meenakshi and Lord Shiva. The other man is Vishnu, Lord Shiva's best man," he said.

His words brought back the memory of a splendid temple I had visited ten days earlier. I searched on my phone: "UNESCO world heritage site," read the Wiki page of the Meenakshi Amman temple. Traveling in India I seldom visited UNESCO sanctioned sites—often crowded with thousands of tourists and lacking any spiritual vibes.

But the Madurai Meenakshi temple would stupefy anyone with its 15 gopurams reaching up to 50 feet in height and two splendid vimanas, the gilded towers in the middle of the structure. This temple was a thing of legends for its mesmerizing beauty.

Meenakshi is known as a very powerful, protective and benevolent Goddess, a form of Lalita Tripura Sundari and Shakti. She is the epitome of wisdom, strength, fertility, love and compassion, who empowers women to be courageous, helping them rise to prominent heights as leaders in society. She is the Goddess of equality and the ultimate protectress of women, much like Vesta.

In a myth, she was considered both a great warrior and the daughter of a Pandya king. She is also described as a very beautiful Goddess with fish-shaped, slanted eyes filled with compassion and benevolence. In Hindu iconography, she is often accompanied by a green parrot that symbolizes love and fertility. And like Vesta, Meenakshi is a very nurturing Goddess.

Traveling with my guru at the beginning of this India trip, I had visited this Madurai temple with a large group of students and felt I had received the blessings of Meenakshi and Shiva.

I now remembered the high frequencies emanating from both the temple and the statues of many deities. In a store near the temple, I had even bought a beautiful brass statue of Meenakshi, asking a priest to bless it in a hydration ceremony. I watched him pour water and milk on the statuette, and then, with a final splash, he rinsed it and handed it back to me. Meenakshi's brass form sparkled, looked alive, and radiated great beauty.

Visiting the sanctum of Meenakshi was strictly forbidden to foreigners, but that day, we had witnessed a miracle. We were mostly

Caucasians, and several among us stood out for their light blond hair—so there was no chance we could pass as Indians.

Yet, for some mysterious reason, the guards at the door let us in. This privilege was unprecedented or very rare, as we later heard from the surprised guides that accompanied us.

In this temple, Meenakshi was the supreme deity, and only after visiting her sanctum sanctorum were you permitted to enter the sanctum of Sundareswarar, her handsome husband Shiva.

Remembering the Most Beautiful Goddess Temple

As we walked to the car, the guide explained: "We are taking you to the Meenakshi temple tomorrow."

Although I felt dizzy from hunger and fatigue, I excitedly considered my good luck for visiting this temple twice in two weeks.

I suddenly felt that seeing the picture of this Goddess on the restaurant wall was no coincidence. Rather, I was certain that my higher-self had orchestrated this opportunity. And it was not a religious site calling me, rather a higher cosmic being was sending me an invitation.

Since I was on a trip to change my karma, the Goddess was reminding me that I am God, a Goddess. In fact, just as the yogis teach us, we are all divine. And she was removing my forgetfulness—and the worst karma of all, limitation.

As I discussed the trip to Madurai with my guide, he advised me to abandon hope of entering the temple. "I will walk in and pray for you because foreigners are not allowed in the sanctum," he said. I told him that I had already visited the temple and sanctum. He seemed very surprised.

It was at this same moment that I began a mental conversation with Meenakshi. I asked her, or rather begged her, to let me visit her in the sanctum sanctorum. My resolve was set in stone, as my heart could not accept any other possibility. And that evening, during the drive back to the hotel in Kumbakonam I could think of nothing else.

I continued to plead with Meenakshi:

Goddess, I came all the way to India to see you in person. Please allow me to enter your sanctum again. Why else would you put this desire in my heart? I want to see you. I need your empowerment for the work I want to do. I cannot leave India without the fulfillment of this wish. And I want to do your rituals in person, as my Nadi palm leaves suggested.

The Nadi tablets were written for me over a thousand years ago by Agastya, the greatest sage and Siddha of all time. In no way could I accept prayers by another person—not even by an experienced history professor like my guide. The omniscient sage Agastya knew that I would need these remedies and prescribed the rituals to be performed at this particularly powerful temple.

At dusk, we reached the hotel. In my room, I lit an incense and placed it in front of the statue of Meenakshi. "Please say yes, so not even man-made rules can stop me from entering your sacred temple," I prayed out loud.

My room was beautiful despite a light coat of dust that seemed to penetrate every barrier. Everyone on the hotel staff seemed calm and not rushed. I longed to live this way, in a place where no one seemed worried or frantic in their daily tasks. And this was one of my favorite aspects of life in South India. That peace, even amidst chaos, was missing in the West.

I loved the traditional Indian décor in the hotel, especially the elegant ebony and brass-studded front door of my bungalow. The thick polished wood, it's beautiful and detailed carving, and double leaves embellished with heavy brass-ring knockers—reminded me more of the Mysore royal palace than the four-star resort it actually was.

As I am remembering and writing this before dawn on a mid-December day, I am at home in the Hudson Valley in New York state, and the early snow has turned to ice. The stars are still shining bright in the clear winter air. And suddenly, taken by melancholic nostalgia for India, I walked to the kitchen to make myself a cup of sweet milky chai. I am now relishing its cinnamon and cardamom scents.

So back in India, in the hotel's garden, I watched countless birds chirping, happily flying over the tall trees by the swimming pool. The air filled with their joyous activities, accompanied by a gentle, divine breeze. I looked at the soft pink clouds quickly turning pale grey, then purple ink after a glorious sunset.

I also noticed a pretty courtyard with a traditional, sacred tulsi plant. Everywhere in India, Tulsi or holy basil was considered a Goddess—sacred to the preserver God Vishnu. This plant radiated celestial frequencies of perfect health, wealth and spiritual bliss.

The birds, the colors in the sky, the gentle breeze, and the tulsi plant were auspicious omens, and I confidently thought:

Tomorrow, I will be the only westerner entering Meenakshi's sanctum sanctorum.

But my certainty disappeared in the morning, as I anxiously waited for both my driver and the guide to pick me up. In the breakfast room, a lovely brass statue of the elephant-headed Ganesha about 30-inch-tall, rested majestically atop a 5-foot pedestal.

As a quick hydration ritual and prayer, I dipped my right ring finger in the clean glass of water on my table and placed the drop on Ganesha's forehead.

Then I stepped outside and from a tree in the garden, I picked a red hibiscus flower sacred to Ganesha. I placed it at his feet and prayed mentally: *Remove all the obstacles from my trip to Madurai. I must visit the Goddess.*

Silently, several waiters had stopped to observe me. An Indian couple sitting at a food-covered table also looked at me curiously. I knew that despite my Indian-style kurti and matching pants, I still looked very much like a foreigner.

Outside I walked on the pretty patio and sat down at an empty table, scanning the surroundings for omens and signs of the future outcome. I sipped my chai and nervously took pictures of the traditional statues of ducks and an impressively tall elephant. Then I stood up, opened a new bottle of mineral water and poured it on the head of the elephant statue as an offering. Again, I prayed to Ganesha.

Asking for a Miracle

On my way out, I looked again at the lush gardens. In the early morning sun, plants and flowers were receiving a refreshing bath from some weak sprinklers. But in the central courtyard a wilted tulsi plant looked sad and called for my attention. It was evident that it desperately needed water, and I felt the plant's pain as it telepathically communicated with me.

I walked up to the plant, and I was horrified at what I saw. In a plain terracotta pot, a few stems of sacred tulsi stood amid chunks of cracked, parched soil—the color of sand rather than a rich brown. Considering the frail looking tulsi, I hoped the plant could be saved.

I promptly took a new bottle of water from my bag, poured some of it into the pot, and recited a mantra. This, I believed brought me the blessings of the holy basil and Vishnu for a successful outcome of my pilgrimage that day.

A young hotel employee wearing a black and white uniform walked by. I asked him if he would help care for the Tulsi plant. He promised he would tell the gardeners to water the Tulsi regularly, and he smiling took a tip.

I was now peaceful again and certain that this would be a memorable, happy day.

The Resplendent Abode of the Goddess

It was a hot day when we arrived in Madurai. At the outskirts of the multicolored temple, I tensely looked at a quarter-mile long line of people waiting at the entrance. This was a bad sign. The military guards would probably allow only local people in the temple, not me.

When my guide and I finally made it past the long queue of pilgrims, we walked into the magnificent Meenakshi temple, and my eyes widened at its splendor.

Probably thanks to my long meditation in the car on our way to the temple, my consciousness seemed more receptive to divinity. Meditation, in fact, can make your observation more acute and sensitive to subtle energies. Even the architecture seemed grander and more beautiful than ever.

My heart fluttered with the desire to enter the sanctum, and the anticipation was wearing my patience. My head began spinning from the warm, dusty air, and I inhaled the thick scent of thousands of fresh flowers—pink, red, white, yellow, orange—overflowing from a myriad of plates in the hands of the multitude of visitors, offerings to Meenakshi. A pleasant perfume of vibhuti, the sacred ash, strengthened the impression that you were stepping onto heavenly grounds.

But my guide burst this spiritual bubble and prepared me for disappointment. "*Ma'am, wait for me here. I will return after the rituals,*" he said.

In my thoughts, I cried:

Never! I will only visit the Goddess in person. I am Indian in my heart, and the Goddess does not care about my nationality.

In tears, my forehead perspiring from the intense heat, I felt my heart filling with rebellion, and I could not give up my hope.

But wait, was that priest really calling me with his arm waving in the air? He was. Incredulous, I followed his instructions to enter a separate, much-faster lane, and we left hundreds of devotees waiting on the left side. Sad for them, I looked back and felt their exhaustion and impatience.

Without any other obstacle in our way, my guide and I followed the priest and walked through a cordoned pathway straight into the Goddess' sanctum. It took me some time to realize this miracle.

Certainly, I did not look Indian, yet there I was in front of another priest asking me my name and Moon constellation—a significant astrological detail. I said out loud the Sanskrit words in one quick breath, "Lalitha, Bharani." I hoped he would not detect my foreign accent. In the sanctum, from an advantageous position I could see the Goddess without any obstructions—a great rarity. I stood there in childlike joy.

Through my knowledge of Vedic astrology, I had chosen an auspicious time for this visit to Meenakshi's temple—and I knew that on this day the positive alignments of the Moon, Mars and the Sun could fulfill my wishes. I handed to the priest my offerings for the Goddess: a beautiful garland of flowers, and a platter with a coconut, sacred powders and fruits. I had purchased these items from an old male vendor at the temple's entrance.

I entered an altered state of consciousness, feeling deeply loved and accepted in that sacred place. Countless voices chanted mysterious mantras, and I watched the light of the ghee lamps that the priests circled around the gorgeous Meenakshi statue. The sounds of sacred bells contributed to my blissful state, perhaps due to the energy of the Goddess herself. I certainly believed so.

My head began to spin again, as if I were about to faint. Despite the sheer joy, this otherworldly atmosphere barely supported my body weakened by traveling and jet-lag.

In my inner vision, I saw that scores of Gods had come to worship the Goddess. Then some desperate devotees, unable to see the life-size statue of Meenakshi, pushed me from behind, making their way forward to get a glimpse of the Goddess in her glorious attire. I moved to the side.

A priest came through the crowd holding a high flame meaning the culmination of the rituals. It was done—the Goddess had blessed everyone with love and miracle-making energy. My higher self and Goddess within had connected with the Goddess without.

Dizzy for the need of fresh air, I moved away from the crowd. Another priest handed me a full basket of blessed offerings—the holy prasad made of fruit, a broken coconut and flowers.

Then holding out a huge, splendid garland made of fresh flowers, he invited me to wear it. I lifted it above my head and placed it around my neck—it was heavy and reached my knees.

I felt as though I was being coronated in the presence of the Divine Mother. I felt infinite gratitude for my fulfilled wish—I had been accepted by the Goddess in her divine palace, and tears began to flow.

I could now visit Lord Shiva, her consort. Soon after the rituals at the Shiva sanctum sanctorum, another priest handed me another very long garland studded with many fresh buds. I was now wearing both garlands, and feeling immensely gratified for this very special honor.

But the Goddess had more surprises in store for me.

The Grand Finale

Still inside the Madurai temple, I was nearly numb from fatigue, when another priest handed me a silky green and red cloth as a gift from the Goddess. Lifting up the two garlands I placed the cloth around my neck. It looked like a long scarf that reached my mid-thighs. I now resembled Meenakshi herself, covered in flowers and shiny fabric. Tears of bliss and gratitude kept rolling freely down my cheeks.

My spiritual connection with Goddess Meenakshi had been strengthened beyond words, and I knew I would never forget this extraordinary day. Although my body felt extremely tired, I remained in an altered state of bliss for the rest of the day.

I desperately needed rest, and I was relieved when we finally reached the hotel that night. Strangely upon seeing me, the concierge ran out from the counter and met me halfway. Now I was shocked.

What does he want?

He then smiled and announced that my room reservation had been upgraded free of charge. Replacing my double room was now a spacious three-room suite, with a gigantic bathroom, and even a large dressing room.

This luxurious gift came without any request from me. My beautiful apartment, comfortable and quiet, acted as an additional healing balm after the 4-hour drive from the temple.

I called room service and ordered an omelet and a bottle of mango juice. After dinner, I fell into a peaceful, uninterrupted sleep until the next morning.

When I flew home to New York a week later, without much thought, I stepped onto the white scale in my bathroom. There was another surprise: I had lost 10 pounds—another prayer answered. Meenakshi, the Goddess of beauty, had helped me become slender again.

Try This

- Download a picture or buy a statue of Meenakshi Amman. Bathe it with clean water, and then pour milk or rose water on the statue. Again, rinse it with water. Dry with a clean cloth. Offer a candle.
- Sit quietly and meditate on her. See her perfect beauty, a sweet smile, and a green parrot symbolizing love sitting on her shoulder.
- Say out loud: "I welcome you. Thank you for your gifts of inspiration, beauty, and prosperity. Thank you for teaching me about sovereignty. You are first before Shiva. Welcome.
- Every day, say out loud this affirmation: "I am filled with the vibrations of the Sacred Feminine. I am the power of the electromagnetic field of the Earth and the embodiment of Goddess love."
- Give yourself a Goddess Day. Buy and wear a beautiful ruby-colored dress or shirt. Buy flowers and wear them in your hair. Affirm that you're beautiful, creative and powerful.
- For men: buy a red shirt or polo, or treat yourself to a spa day with a relaxing massage or swimming. Affirm that you're handsome, creative and powerful.

CHAPTER 7

THE MYSTERY OF MARY MAGDALENE

You are already getting the Goddess' energy inside. She is your intelligence, but it has not been activated. The Goddess lives in the golden 1000-petalled lotus of your subtle body, which corresponds to your brain. -Dr. Pillai

I woke up in the Brahma Muhurta—between 3:30 a.m. and 4 a.m.—also called the time of the Creator God. The yogis purposely rise in these early morning hours to achieve higher states of consciousness.

During the day, a thought had returned multiple times with the desire to learn the truth about Mary Magdalene. By projecting my consciousness and focusing on one goal, I have often received knowledge from the Akash or ether—information that I had neither researched nor studied. So, I repeated this experiment, and kept asking: Who are you, Mary Magdalene?

Still awake at 4 a.m., I now wondered about her life and her role in the life of Yeshua or Jesus. After meditating, still in the dark of night, I was inspired to write some pages of this book. Then again, I asked: "God, reveal to me the truth about Mary Magdalene."

I entered a deep meditation. At some point, a profound answer came:

She was a spiritual master, a Goddess of deep love and mercy, whose ministry went a long way to spread Yeshua's teachings to the world.

I felt this was the truth and thought:

If this answer is true, the recorded history of Mary Magdalene was false.

Then, the confusion must have started on Easter Sunday of 591 AD, when the world's perception of Mary Magdalene changed forever. This event also lead to catastrophic consequences for both women in religion and our connection to the Divine Feminine.

The catalyst for this unfortunate change was a sermon by Pope Gregory, who singlehandedly obfuscated Mary Magdalene's true identity, her central role in both Jesus' life and early Christianity, and her transformative ministry.

The Pope, in fact, had mistaken Mary Magdalene for another woman who had anointed Jesus' feet and was believed to be a sex worker.

The Pope's sermon, turning Mary Magdalene into a prostitute overnight, may appear more like a sneak attack on female spirituality than actual confusion. And due to his choice of words, Mary Magdalene suddenly acquired the mistaken identity of a sinful Mary of Bethany.

Dark History

Given the power of the Pope at that time, Mary Magdalene quickly became a sinful woman in the collective mind. Although her reputation was cleared by another Pope 1,500 years later, it was too late.

In fact, even today, many people imagine a shadow of seduction and sin around Mary Magdalene. In the Renaissance, too, she was invariably portrayed as a naked woman in sensual, suggestive poses.

Also, historically, the Church was known to have covered up many truths by banning the gnostic texts, persecuting and killing the Gnostics, wiping the historical records of the Essenes, persecuting and killing the Cathars, calling "idolatry" the rituals of other religions, and more.

And, over the centuries the Church persecuted women to unprecedented extents during the various Inquisitions and countless witchcraft trials, leading to the torture and murder of at least 300,000 women. Most of the time, these innocents were killed for simply praying to a Goddess or using healing herbal compounds.

The Inquisitions also caused the deaths of many men accused of sorcery, and so the bloodshed and terror continued for centuries. Moreover, the Church suppressed, imprisoned or killed thinkers, philosophers, and even scientists—such as Galileo Galilei—who reached conclusions that the Church found unacceptable. After all, Galilei's only fault was to prove that the Earth was round and rotated around the Sun.

Also, by suppressing Mary Magdalene, a woman, and elevating the mother of Jesus, a virgin, the Church's authorities de facto put a judgment on women's life and sexuality—portraying any non-virgin woman as potentially impure.

But Jesus carried no prejudice towards women at a time when women depended on their fathers, brothers and husbands for their livelihoods and life choices. So, the idea that a woman could become an important figure in the life of Jesus and in his ministry must have been inadmissible for the religious hierarchies.

But then, in 1969, the Catholic Church quietly removed from the liturgical calendar the mistaken identity of Mary Magdalene as Mary of Bethany—just a small step after a staggering 19 centuries of slander.

But finally, the truth won in 2016 when Pope Francis elevated Mary Magdalene to the status of "Apostle of all Apostles." And she is now called a saint in several Christian religions.

As for me, I am profoundly sad, even indignant, that a divine woman so close to Jesus—whom he loved deeply—could be characterized as a sex worker for nearly 2,000 years.

Moreover, impressive scholarly research and countless books by intuitive individuals further challenge the Church's official narrative about the relationship between Jesus and Mary. And a central question still lingers: Was Mary Magdalene Jesus' wife?

Interesting Finding

An event supporting the possibility that Jesus was married to Mary occurred in 2012, when Karen L. King, a Harvard Divinity School professor, presented a fragment in the Coptic language of Egypt—often used in ancient gnostic texts.

This small piece of papyrus came from an ancient document containing the words: "Jesus said to them, my wife." While most scholars consider the fragment authentic, others have called it a forgery or found its content too inflammatory to handle.

However, carbon dating found this fragment to be consistent with the time period between the 6th and 9th centuries AD.

The Official Story

In the canonical gospels, Mary Magdalene was mentioned twelve times, more than any other follower. She was described as a woman who traveled with Jesus and the other apostles, witnessed the crucifixion and death of Jesus, and was the first person to meet him after his resurrection. And, according to the canonical Gospel of Luke, Mary Magdalene was a wealthy woman who financially supported Jesus' ministry.

The Golden Legend

Around the year 1260 an Italian archbishop, Jacobus de Voragine, wrote about Mary Magdalene's high social status and her special relationship with Jesus in the "Golden Legend," which became the most popular medieval book of all time.

But the archbishop, too, held the common belief that when she first met Jesus, Mary Magdalene was an impure woman:

"As she shone in beauty greatly, and in riches, so much the more she submitted her body to delight, and therefore she lost her right name, and was called customably a sinner."

He also wrote that Mary was a royal and incredibly wealthy:

"Mary Magdalene had her surname of Magdala, a castle, and was born of right noble lineage and parents, which were descended of the lineage of kings…She, with her brother Lazarus and her sister Martha, possessed the castle of Magdala, which is two miles from Nazareth, and Bethany, the castle which is nigh to Jerusalem, and also a great part of Jerusalem."

Then the archbishop dropped this bombshell:

"Jesus embraced her all in his love and made her right familiar with him."

My Intuitive Insights

When I was selecting the Goddesses for this book, it was my intuition that inspired me to write about Mary Magdalene. Especially telling was what happened in May 2024 with my previous book "Think and Receive Miracles."

For several days, in fact, my book remained in the top Amazon best sellers in the USA—but behind another book, "Mary Magdalene Revealed" by Harvard-trained theologian Meggan Watterson, which was consistently the number one best seller.

Then, a miracle happened. My book rose to number one and "Mary Magdalene Revealed" became number two. So, I could not stop thinking about Mary Magdalene. In addition, I started my research and found "The Golden Legend" by the Italian archbishop. Then, I found for the first time the "Gospel of Mary Magdalene."

Now, I could not ignore her any longer—and I was both intrigued and hooked.

I believe that Mary Magdalene intervened to touch my consciousness and heart, so I would discover her and contribute with this book to bringing back the Shakti in the West.

Farfetched? Not really, because I know from my Vedic studies that not only are higher beings in constant touch with all of us, but they literally live in our unconscious—and there is no separation at all.

Today, I consider Mary both a minister and the companion of Jesus. She was a spiritual master of the highest order, unwavering in her love and faith, and the only apostle who truly understood Yeshua's most profound teachings.

We can find some evidence of all the above in a gnostic text found in Egypt in 1773, the Pistis Sophia. But as often happens with ancient texts, several pages were missing. Could it be that those pages spoke of a marriage between Mary Magdalene and Jesus? No one knows yet.

Written in ancient Greek in 170 AD, the Pistis Sophia described Mary Magdalene as the Christ Sophia, who was born at the same time as Jesus of Nazareth, and was the embodiment of the words of Jesus—or Christ Logos.

In the more ancient Vedic tradition, too, a Goddess embodies the words of the Divine. She is the ethereal Saraswati, who wears a white gown, sits on a white lotus, holds the sacred Vedas, and represents the highest wisdom.

At the start of this book, I intuitively knew that the Christ Consciousness had returned to the Earth plane in conjunction with the start of the Golden Age in December 2023.

And in the last seven years, Jesus has made many appearances in my meditations, even though I had forgotten him, as I preferred the Vedic deities and archetypes. Also, getting reacquainted with Yeshua's original teachings brought me many tears of joy and several extraordinary miracles.

But what was really missing for me was an understanding of how Shakti—as in the duality of Shiva Shakti, or of God the Father and the Mother Goddess—was connected with Jesus. And that is when the preeminence of Mary Magdalene was revealed to me—I realized that she was Shakti in Jesus' life.

This is relevant today, as many spiritual teachers now believe that Jesus has a central role in our current spiritual awakening, as we ascend to the 5th dimension. What is happening is that we are becoming a frequency match for the Christ Consciousness, accepting our divine origins, and realizing that heaven on earth is possible.

Our increasing awareness of the Goddess is also facilitating the return of mass-scale love, compassion, forgiveness, and freedom from fear. So, embracing the Pistis Sophia as a true narration about Jesus and Mary Magdalene as a divine couple makes more sense to me.

Another Intuitive Insight

My intuition says that the missing pages of the Pistis Sophia shined light on the central role of Mary Magdalene in Jesus' life. Those missing pages, then, would be crucial to learn the secrets of Mary's ministry—which certainly contributed to raising the consciousness during ancient times.

Thanks to her shakti—which is primarily connected with Creation—she helped us realize that "heaven on earth" exists right here, right now. And, although this earthly heaven exceeds the light spectrum visible to our human eyes, we can experience it by raising our consciousness and connecting with the Goddess.

Today, Mary Magdalene and millions of other Goddesses, the embodiments of pure divine femininity, have returned to empower us, so we can free ourselves, and put an end to hatred, division and evil, and restore justice on Earth.

Although we might see Mary as an enigmatic and mysterious figure, she was actually the most mentioned disciple in all canonical and gnostic texts.

In my view, the three gnostic Gospels of Thomas, Philip, and Mary Magdalene serve as indisputable evidence that not only was Mary a pure-hearted, well-educated woman, but also Jesus' favorite apostle.

Moreover, according to ascetic Gnostics, Mary Magdalene belonged to a royal lineage of Goddess worshippers and was a priestess from the lineage of female adepts called the "Marys."

Asking for the Truth and More Answers

Intuitive revelations on Mary Magdalene have been flowing into my consciousness since the start of this book. By allowing these visions into my awareness, I realized that I could view past events, and—when it was possible to verify their accuracy from known data, my remote viewing proved correct each time. I was stunned by the clarity and truth in my visions.

The future, too, seemed available and came in glimpses during my meditations. Often, I learned about my life in the future, and even seemingly small details came true.

You could try to play and "imagine" your past life. Whatever you say and feel may turn out to be true. There is always a reason why you choose a certain time period and not another. And certainly, something in your imaginings holds true for your soul.

Our doubts, in fact, come from the heavy conditioning we have experienced since childhood, from educational institutions, our family, acquaintances, and our environment—which together build the so-called consensus reality.

The mind, too, operates as per a "negativity bias" that doubts everything we cannot touch with our senses—like the soul, the Goddess, and our intuition—which the yogis consider the highest intelligence.

Today, I prayed out loud to Jesus: "Yeshua, please tell me the truth about Mary Magdalene and your teachings." Within a few minutes, searching online, a telling synchronicity occurred when my eyes fell on a video with an irresistible title: "The Vatican's Suppression of Jesus' Forbidden Teachings."

Synchronicity often manifests at astonishing speed. I clicked randomly in the middle of the video and heard a man say:

"Jesus didn't have only 12 apostles. He had 24—and 12 of them were women."

At these words, I felt tingling all over my body—one of the ways I receive intuition about something truthful and profound. The speaker was a podcast guest, an author and a historian of Jesus. I thanked Yeshua out loud.

The guest then said, "Mary Magdalene was Yeshua's soulmate, his Twin Flame."

In India, a deeply sacred union between two cosmic higher beings can be found in the Vedas, Puranas and Upanishads.

Not only did I believe what the podcast guest had said, but I remembered that this union of Jesus and Mary was also described in the Gospel of Thomas and the Gospel of Mary Magdalene.

Mary's Divine Role

I was recently mesmerized by the beautiful movie "Mary Magdalene." In this 2018 film, she appeared much closer to Jesus than in other movies. Away from the other apostles, the two of them would sit together on a mountain, discussing spiritual truths, often remaining in deep silence. A certain otherworldly intimacy transpired from their interactions.

I read the canonical Gospels when I was a child, around age 7, and I loved them so much that I reread them multiple times. But as an adult, after seeing movies about Jesus' life, I have been wondering why the Gospels never revealed much about the Resurrection. My thoughts invariably were:

Were there no intuitive seers at that time? What did Jesus Christ look like in his light body? What did he reveal to the apostles when he spoke to them after the Resurrection? What happened after?

So, all movies about the Savior's life seemed disappointing to me. Were there no movie directors willing to show some imaginative scenes of spiritual light and ascension?

Despite the available special effects, and sci-fi technology showing countless space travels, futuristic machines, scary looking ETs, all kinds of wars, and bloody violence, could they not show us a light body or what happened after the Resurrection?

Apparently, fiction never dared to explore these sacred themes, as all movies invariably ended at Jesus' death—putting a symbolic end to his life mission as the Savior.

The scenes clearly displayed the film directors' obsessions with the Christ's wounds, his agony and the last scene as he bled to death. Of course, his sacrifice of the flesh and blood were central themes. But the movies suggested nothing about the extraordinary transformation and freedom that Yeshua's sacrifice brought to humanity.

After a few inevitable shots of a crying Mother Mary and the overturned burial boulder, it was "The End." Was this due to religious dogma or a general lack of interest in spiritual enlightenment among film-makers? Probably both.

So, imagine my incredulity and happiness when I found the Pistis Sophia that filled this huge spiritual gap. This text was a paradigm shifter for me: it finally described a resurrected Jesus—the risen Savior with Mary Magdalene at his side.

This sacred gnostic text revealed that after his Resurrection, Jesus spent eleven years talking to his disciples, revealing many mysteries. This book also highlighted Mary Magdalene's sacred role in the Savior's teachings to the apostles. After Jesus Christ had acquired more spiritual power and a "garment" of light—he was then able to reveal even deeper secrets about many unknown cosmologies.

In addition, the Pistis Sophia disclosed Mary Magdalene's intimate relationship with Jesus Christ, and contained many mesmerizing descriptions of his light body.

Can you imagine interacting daily with Jesus? One moment you are talking to a man of flesh and blood. Next, you are witnessing his transformation into a garment of light, the same that you, too, can acquire by following his ministry.

I believe that the shakti or divine femininity of Mary Magdalene contributed to making Yeshua's teachings the most profound in the last 2,000 years. Like the Vedic archetype Shiva, who was one with his wife Parvati, Jesus expressed his spiritual powers through the help of his beloved Mary Magdalene.

I can imagine Mary's deep emotion in seeing her loved one in a light form. The light-body transformation is a theme I have explored for many years in mystery school studies with Dr. Pillai. Through the stories of the Tamil Siddha yogis of India, I learned of their ability to turn their bodies into light and ascend to higher planes of existence. In the Pistis Sophia, the descriptions of Jesus' light body resonated with my soul, and brought me longing for ascension to a higher dimension.

If you feel emotional thinking about your physical body turning into light in the "blink of an eye," perhaps you have already experienced this in a past life. Emotion, in fact, is the language of the soul and it helps you remember your soul's experiences.

Mariam and the Savior

In the following verses of the Pistis Sophia, Mary Magdalene is "Mariam the beautiful," with a lovely speaking voice and perfect words.

"That light-power, however, came down upon Jesus and it surrounded him completely as he was sitting at a distance from his disciples, and he gave light exceedingly, there being no measure to the light which was his. And the disciples did not see Jesus because of the great light in which he was, or which was his, for their eyes were darkened because of the great light in which he was. But they only saw the light which cast forth many rays of light. And the rays of light were not equal to one another…

"Now when he had said these things to his disciples, he said to them: 'He who has ears to hear, let him hear.' Now it happened when Mariam heard these words as the Savior was saying them, she stared for one hour into the air and said: 'My Lord, command me that I speak openly'…".

What Jesus Said

"Mariam, you blessed one, whom I will complete in all the mysteries of the height, speak openly. You are she whose heart is more directed to the Kingdom of Heaven than all your brothers."

Then, Mariam spoke and asked advanced questions on cosmology, astrology, and astronomy.

"Excellent, Mariam. You are blessed beyond all women upon earth, because you shall be the powerful divine abode of all divine abodes..."

Now my thoughts reflected incredible surprise, like an awakening of sorts:

Oh my God! Did Jesus say that Mary Magdalene was the greatest heaven of all heavens, the refuge of all refuges for the devotees?

According to some gnostic ascetics of the late 1st century, he did. And Jesus lovingly spoke to Mary Magdalene as to an equal, which implied both a closeness and an affinity he did not have with the other apostles.

The Golden Diary

The 13th-century text called the Golden Legend, or rather the "Golden Diary," changed the collective mind in medieval times.

In some pages, Mary Magdalene was described with awe as a saint who spent the last 30 years of her life as a hermit, like a yogi, in a cave outside of Marseilles, France. The author said that Angels carried Mary Magdalene to Heaven seven times a day so she could hear the choir of celestial beings.

"So, filled day by day with this exquisite heavenly fare, when she was brought back to her cave, she had not the slightest need for bodily nourishment."

Like innumerable yogis of India, Mary Magdalene had acquired the supernormal ability to sustain her body without food or water and receive nourishment directly from divine light stimulating the "medulla oblongata" in the brain.

The True Nature of Mary Magdalene

Beautifully channeled information from "The Sophia Code" reveals that Mary Magdalene had undergone extensive studies in Essene mystery schools, thanks to the influence of her evolved father, an Essene himself. Most likely, Jesus' teachings were also influenced by the Essenes.

In addition, during their multiple trips to India and Egypt, Mary received great teachings from different spiritual masters. All this was beyond remarkable in the Middle East 2,000 years ago, when women were repressed, marginalized, and often persecuted by unscrupulous men.

But Mary Magdalene enjoyed exceptional freedoms, acquired incredible spiritual knowledge, and was highly qualified to empower other disenfranchised women. And I believe she did.

In the writings of many authors, we can sense her extraordinary courage, strength and deep love for Jesus. For example, when all the other apostles fled from the crucifixion and refused to witness Jesus' painful death, Mary Magdalene remained. Led by her divine compassion and accompanied by Mother Mary and a few other women, she stayed close to Jesus even during those tragic moments.

More importantly, she was the first person who found the empty tomb, and Jesus appeared to her first. "Mary," he called her affectionately. He then instructed her to reveal his ascension to the other apostles.

Overjoyed, she recognized him at once. It is remarkable how Jesus entrusted her with this important task—to alert the other disciples and give them the good news about his resurrection. I believe that this episode alone would place her in an exalted role in Jesus' life and grant her a highly divine status.

Paradigm Shift: The Gospel of Mary Magdalene

The original manuscript of the Gospel of Mary Magdalene was found in 1896 in Cairo, Egypt. As it happened with the Pistis

Sophia, many pages were missing on its discovery. Was someone, perhaps, trying to hide the truth about Mary Magdalene, and withholding the full contents of this gnostic gospel? I believe so.

Those missing pages might have revealed some deep truths about Mary's pure nature and her paramount role as the Sacred Feminine in the life of Jesus—much like Shiva Shakti.

Was a Vatican envoy responsible for stealing such controversial pages? Again, I believe so. Fortunately, we can find enough information in the Gospel of Mary Magdalene that can forever change our religious views.

The gospel's initial six pages are missing, and page seven begins with questions from disciples to Mary Magdalene after the Resurrection of Jesus Christ.

"Teach us about the material world," they said to the Savior. Jesus explained to them profound truths about sin and the pure, original nature of humanity.

On page ten, Peter spoke:

Sister, we know that you are greatly loved by the Savior, more than any other woman. Tell us those words of His that you remember, the things which you know and we don't, the teachings we never heard.

Mary answered, saying: What is hidden from you I shall reveal to you. Whatever is unknown to you, and I remember, I will tell you.

She spoke: 'Once I saw the Lord in a vision and I said to him: Now I see you in this vision. He answered me and said: Blessed are you Mary, for you do not waver at the sight of me. How wonderful you are! For this is where the treasure lies.'

But Andrew responded and said to the brothers and sisters: 'Tell me, what do you think about all that she has been telling us? Say what you will, but I, for one, don't believe that the Savior would have said such things! Certainly, these are unorthodox teachings, it all seems quite different from his way of thinking.'

After some consideration, Peter responded in a similar way. He questioned the brothers about the Savior: 'Did he really speak secretly with a woman and not openly so that we could all hear? Are we just going to turn around and listen to her? Did he really choose her and prefer her to us? Surely, he wouldn't have wanted to show that she is more worthy than we are?'

Peter had openly defied Mary Magdalene, and she began crying. But another disciple came to her rescue:

Levi responded to Peter, saying: 'Peter, you have always been hot-tempered from the beginning, and now we see you arguing against this woman as though you were her adversary.'

'Yet if the Savior deemed her worthy, indeed if he himself has made her worthy, then who are you to despise and reject her? Surely the Savior's appraisal of her is completely reliable. That is why he loved her more than us.'

Peter had admitted that Jesus loved Mary Magdalene deeply, more than any other woman.

And Levi had said, "He loved her more than us."

LALITHA DONATELLA RIBACK

My Experience with Dogma

After several years of living in the USA, I returned to Italy on vacation. One day, I decided to visit a Renaissance church in Bergamo, near my parents' house.

I observed the lovely, framed artworks by renowned Renaissance artists. A beautiful statue of Mother Mary with silver rays emanating from her head touched my heart. I stopped to look in awe as she radiated so much love.

This church's peaceful and cool environment calmed my emotions, and I enjoyed the pervasive scent of incense, the sacred ornaments and the impressive architecture. I suddenly felt I needed to kneel and pray.

On my way out, I stopped to say hello to the pastor. He seemed distracted, absent, and during our short conversation, I mentioned my marriage to an American Jewish man.

Suddenly, the priest became animated. With a stern look in his eyes and an angry tone, he said: "You have committed a grave sin." I answered, "A sin?"

His brief reply left me speechless. "For a Catholic person, the marriage to someone from another religion is a sin against God."

I thought, *but this is absolutely ridiculous, and I stopped short from telling him the same.* With a sour feeling in my heart, I left and realized the uselessness of offering a contrary view to someone so embedded in doctrine.

The old ugly "us versus them" so common in different religions had resurfaced, and in that place I no longer found anything honoring my beliefs in the universality of God's mercy, and Jesus' all-embracing love.

Mary Magdalene as Jesus' Twin Flame

I consider myself a follower of Yeshua. I love him very much, and his teachings have made a powerful return into my life with his unprompted appearances in my meditations. These visions have had a lasting impact, and I tearfully remembered that, when I was about 3 to 4 years old, he appeared and played with me.

I now believe that Yeshua was:
- The greatest prophet—but not the only one
- An adept yogi and master, who, in his youth, studied in several mystery schools in India and Egypt
- An adept Essene, and a powerful spiritual healer
- An experienced exorcist
- A divine miracle maker
- An incarnation of the Divine Masculine
- One of the most loving and compassionate beings to ever walk on Earth

The following stems from my intuitions and meditations, as well as the knowledge I received from my Guru. Additionally, I have done extensive research into the Bible, the canonical Gospels, and the gnostic Gospel of Mary Magdalene, and the Gospel of Philip.

According to my spiritual teacher, Mary Magdalene traveled with the blood of Jesus in a chalice, with the intention of spreading its powers and blessings to many places in the Middle East and Europe, including the island of Malta and France.

Mary's life-changing ideas included personal sovereignty for all—including women—a direct experience of the sacred mysteries of the Holy Spirit and a deep union with the divine beyond the medium of the religious authorities.

In addition, she gave women access to deep spiritual mysteries once reserved for men. Also, she courageously embraced her supporting role next to Jesus, helping women and men understand his true teachings, such as:

- Miracle making
- Transubstantiation of bread and wine into flesh and blood
- Light body
- Ascension
- Holy Spirit

Who Feared the Power of Mary Magdalene?

Even in mainstream Christianity, Mary Magdalene held a privileged spiritual status. For example, three canonical gospels mentioned her first before all the other apostles.

The apostle Luke also said that Jesus cured Mary Magdalene of demonic possession, extracting seven demons from her body. But few know that at that time, both physical and mental illnesses were believed to be caused by demons. So, the canonical Gospel of Luke did not necessarily imply sins of the flesh, as some people seem to believe.

Also, during the life of Mary Magdalene, women were considered evil or possessed by demons simply for not following the mores of their society, demanding marriage and offspring.

Beatings and persecution of women by male family members were all too common. These terrible conditions must have caused much sorrow and mental agony to women like Mary, who desired a different path.

And I believe that the apostle Philip, in the gnostic Gospel of Philip, went a long way to restore truth when he said:

- Jesus loved Mary Magdalene the most.
- Mary was considered Jesus' companion.
- Jesus would kiss her on the lips, causing the jealousy of other apostles.
- Before anyone else, Mary Magdalene witnessed the Resurrection.
- Jesus entrusted her to carry out the most delicate task of announcing his transformation into a heavenly body.

Since the Gnostics were pure ascetics and did not seek any political or religious powers, it is easier to believe these accounts revealing the holy role of Mary Magdalene.

As it turned out, Mary was a special disciple and an important female figure within the closest circle of Yeshua. Early on, the Church began calling gnostic teachings "heretic" and in the 6th century, the Pope set out to dishonor Mary Magdalene, placing the label of prostitute on her name—a dishonor that would last for millennia.

So, it is very likely that religious authorities at that time did not like seeing so much spiritual power in the hands of a female figure, especially one so close to Jesus.

It is also extraordinary that the gnostic Gospel of Mary Magdalene remained a legitimate part of the Bible for over one thousand years.

But it was then permanently removed, banned and considered heretic ever since. Today, my heart and my soul are full of gratitude for this divine encounter with Mary Magdalene. I praise her both as a saint, and a Goddess. I ask her to remind all women that they are sovereign Goddesses with the power to live a magnificent soul purpose.

I praise her beauty, courage, divinity and special powers as she returns into our consciousness to be part of the new Golden Age. I know that Mary Magdalene will help restore truth and dignity to both men and women. Amen.

TRY THIS

- Saying the name of a Goddess means bringing her here from the higher dimensions and onto the earth plane. Call on Mary Magdalene and say: "Mary Magdalene, I call on you. Help me experience miracles."
- Imagine Mary Magdalene's joy as she becomes bathed with the light of her beloved, resurrected Yeshua. Visualize the light as it envelopes you. Feel the joy and bliss.
- If you want to experience the power of Yeshua in your life, declare out loud that you are Mary Magdalene. Meditate on this idea and explore it. You might witness incredible transformation.
- Ask Mary Magdalene to infuse you with the power of Jesus to heal, manifest, and transmute. Ask her to help you receive a soulmate relationship—filled with true love, harmony, compatibility, and spiritual union.
- Ask Mary Magdalene to bless you with perfect healing—a healing miracle.
- Ask Mary Magdalene to help you find supreme courage, speaking up in your voice and resist the pressures from those who want you to do wrong. Ask her to help you experience your sovereign power.
- Ask her for the power to connect with your Higher Self and meet with Angels.

- Gratitude attracts and helps you manifest the life you want. Thank Mary Magdalene for coming into your life and bringing you much inspiration and many miracles.

CHAPTER 8

GODDESS RUACH

You have come with a great capital, your soul. This soul has come from God. And God's soul and your soul are not different. -Dr. Pillai

Receive the Spirit of the Goddess. See her enter into the body, mind, and the soul, and stay with this joy. -Dr. Pillai

"The Holy Spirit is a Goddess. Her name is Ruach," said Dr. Pillai during a spiritual retreat in India. My teacher has always had a profound connection with Jesus and the Holy Spirit and encouraged us to ask for the intervention of the Holy Spirit to create miracles—just as Jesus had taught. But I was reluctant to follow this teaching—

it felt so much like Sunday school, the catechism of my childhood. Rather, I wanted to go to a temple and pray to Ganesha.

But then I was floored because my teacher made another revelation:

"If you experience the Holy Spirit, you will have that same power." I could have the power of the Holy Spirit? It seemed too amazing and mind-blowing. But I really wanted to experience miracles. I wanted a bigger house, more travels, the freedom to take a year of vacation to explore my inner self and evolve. This was intriguing to me, so I started to pay more attention.

I learned that the Holy Spirit is inside each of us at all times. She is a powerful Goddess who is omniscient, omnipotent, and omnipresent. Also, Ruach means "breath" in ancient Hebrew. What breath? Divine breath. But also, your own breath, your spirit, and your life, says Dr. Pillai.

What Is Happening Now

The vibrational frequencies of Earth and our galaxy are now increasing and human beings, too, are vibrating faster. This phenomenon is bringing the great spiritual awakening, prophesized a long time ago.

Soon, many people will realize that they are the Holy Spirit—and when our consciousness is awakened, then our vibrations are faster—so we acquire the same power to heal ourselves and others and create any miracle we want. In other words, we are embracing the Christ Consciousness.

For millions of people right now, the teachings of the Holy Spirit are making a comeback—because Jesus will be prominent in the Golden Age, along with the Goddesses and other higher cosmic beings who have returned to our galaxy.

If you do not believe in Jesus, Gods or Goddesses, you can think in terms of sages or benevolent ETs or simply pray to the universe.

Years ago, on the day of the Pentecost—the yearly traditional date when the Holy Spirit comes to Earth—I felt uninspired and skeptical again. Sometimes, Christian liturgy felt dry and unrelatable, and I had no desire to connect with the Holy Spirit.

My experience with Jesus had been different and special—with his direct presence in my childhood when I literally saw him and he spoke to me. He was real. But the Holy Spirit? No, this being felt definitely distant.

But now I was learning that the Holy Spirit was the Divine Feminine—and that spurred a mild interest.

Then I came across a public video of Dr. Pillai in which he said: "Receive the Goddess, the Holy Spirit, into your brain, into all parts of your body, your DNA. Then, you will begin to prophesy and perform miracles. The Holy Spirit will come like a wind."

Now, this was very interesting. I could perform miracles? I could prophesize? I definitely liked these possibilities. The New

Testament, too, mentioned the Holy Spirit as a wind. Easy enough, I thought.

I searched for a biblical quote:

"And suddenly there came a sound from heaven as of a rushing mighty wind, and it filled all the house where they were sitting."

— Acts 2:2

This analogy of the Holy Spirit as a wind still seemed too abstract, so I remained unconvinced. But later that day, as I was relaxing in a state of light meditation, something happened that changed my mind forever.

I was home alone, and I decided to call out loud to the Holy Spirit:

"Holy Spirit, Ruach, I don't know you. Can you give me an experience of your existence?"

Immediately at the sound of these words, a nearby ajar door that led to the garden opened itself wide and then, with a thunderous bang, it closed.

I remained still with my eyes wide open, feeling my fast heartbeat. Although I felt no real fear, I was truly shocked. I had never felt a similar gust of wind coming from that doorway. It was a warm June day with barely any breeze, and until that moment, I could hear outside a sweet chirping of birds playing in the peaceful surroundings.

It is not a windy day, I reasoned.

All the other windows and doors were closed, so the possibility of a sudden gust of wind causing the door to shut itself closed was remote, if not impossible. Also, that was an old, heavy wooden door, thickly made with old artisan techniques—not a hollow one like some modern versions.

When I finally calmed down, I smiled at the incredible speed of the Holy Spirit's answer to my request.

Traveling with Feminine Cosmic Beings

I was standing, like the other meditators, with my eyes closed, arms and hands outstretched in prayer and the palms facing the ceiling. We were chanting a mantra to Goddess Ruach, the Holy Spirit.

The crescendo in our voices, the sacred frequencies from the sounds, brought a tingling sensation in my body, taking me into some kind of transcendental state where there were no apparent thoughts. I felt myself falling into something similar to a vortex, and then I temporarily forgot my body.

Suddenly, behind my closed eyes, shimmering and fluid white and blue forms moved closer to my space—and I intuitively knew they were Goddesses. Soon, I was transported into spirals of light, and a thick, pastel-colored fog descended. When the fog slowly dissipated, the light grew brighter, taking over my entire visual field.

Then I moved through a timeless space, into swirling galaxies with the bodiless luminous female beings. This whole experience took only 10 minutes, perhaps 15, but then I was changed. I opened my eyes, and I knew that something very profound had happened.

I realized that I had an out-of-body experience, similar to the one with Lalita Tripura Sundari. I felt tears of bliss in my eyes. Again, I was completely unprepared for this experience.

But this time the travel in the galaxies was even more significant because I was fully alert, standing, and not lying down on the floor as the first time. So, I was reminded that we are surrounded by higher beings, and only our lack of attention blocks our vision of higher realities.

Apparently, the Holy Spirit was not one Goddess but several.

This experience had happened in a spiritual retreat in Kumbakonam, a divine village that resembled drawings of the classical India of the Chola dynasty—with large gardens inhabited by antique, life-size statues of divine beings from the Vedic tradition—Muruga, Ganesha, the Sun God, Lakshmi, Parvati, Saraswati, and many more.

In the holiness of this atmosphere, accentuated by an intense scent of incense everywhere, it was far easier to let go of limiting preconceptions.

Mohini, the master teacher instructed by Dr. Pillai, was expertly taking us into a meditation to develop a deeper connection with the Holy Spirit Ruach—who for me turned out to be a collective of Goddesses, and not a single holy being.

I had felt so welcome and loved during that short journey with the cosmic female beings. I felt blessed, as if I had received an initiation into their mysteries, as we moved through myriads of pastel-colored wormholes with splashes of white light.

I longed to repeat this experience, and perhaps I have in my sleep—the state where there is no time or space in which we find ourselves in bodiless travels, learning, healing ourselves, and evolving.

Again, I had realized that we are neither the body nor the mind—and more importantly, we are surrounded by higher benevolent beings, who are loving and can help us transform ourselves.

When we learn that we are not limited to the body-mind and our current perception of reality—we can create miraculous new opportunities and happiness.

However, during the day we often become deeply involved in meaningless activities—missing divine signs, intuitive revelations, and great opportunities. And in our chaotic pursuit of simpler goals, we forget that we are divine.

So, it is important to remain alert, notice signs of divine guidance, and use them to transform your life into a more desirable reality. And although the Goddesses live in us, we risk missing their life-altering messages and wonderful miracles.

So, embracing the presence of the Goddess Ruach can change your life, empower you, make you sovereign, more peaceful, more loving, wealthier, more beautiful, kinder, and totally free.

Our Misunderstanding of the Lord's Prayer and the Sacred Feminine

Unfortunately, the Lord's Prayer in today's version has never been my favorite invocation. And now I know why.

As a matter of fact, Jesus spoke Aramaic, and neither English nor Latin. So, the word "Father" in the Lord's Prayer is not supposed to be masculine at all—because in the original Aramaic its meaning is a combination of masculine and feminine: Father Mother.

Dr. Neil Douglas-Klotz, a scholar in religious studies, has translated many teachings of Jesus from the original Aramaic. The original meaning of the Lord's Prayer in Aramaic would make no sense if we read it through the lenses of religious doctrine.

"Our Father, who art in heaven," in its pre-religious form as spoken by Jesus, was actually "Abwoon D'bashmaya," meaning "Oh Birther, Father, Mother of the cosmos."

The prayer continues with the following, "Hallowed be thy name," which is an incorrect translation from the original Aramaic meaning, "You create all that moves in light."

So, the correct Aramaic meaning is, "Father Mother of the Cosmos, You create all that moves in light."

I find the original Aramaic meaning much more beautiful and profound—and a far cry from the version we use today. In fact, these simple original words include the presence of a loving Divine Feminine. And this is why Jesus' original words seem much more complete and closer to the truth.

Try This

- Make a resolution that you will remain open and receptive to divine experiences with the Divine Feminine.
- Expect miracles and life-changing revelations.
- Ruach is love. Find ways to embody love in your life. Be love.
- Call on the Holy Spirit by extending out your arms with your palms up towards the ceiling, and say "Ruach, Ruach, Ruach, bless me with this…" ask for a miracle. Ask for guidance or a relationship, a gift of money, a new job, spiritual enlightenment, or anything else that matters to you.
- Be at one with the Holy Spirit. Become one with her love and light. She is your Mother who wants you to be absolutely happy and fulfilled.
- Thank the Holy Spirit.

CHAPTER 9

RAKAKSHI AND THE WISH-FULFILLING GEM

Sacred Woman consciousness is the ultimate answer to planetary healing. - Joseph Campbell

Once upon a time, millions of years ago, an extraterrestrial female being of great power lived on the small island of Rameshwaram, in the Indian Ocean. People considered her a Goddess, a highly benevolent being who blessed righteous people with many miracles. Her name was Rakakshi.

In addition to her supernormal powers and extraordinary beauty, Rakakshi owned a very powerful divine technology— the Chintamani gem that fulfilled all wishes—which was probably a meteorite-based instrument from another galaxy. The Chintamani included properties of healing, manifesting, and bestowing spiritual growth. Some myths say that the Chintamani originally came from Sirius, a binary star system.

In time, the Goddess left the Earth—and people built a temple in her honor. However, her light body and subtle energy are still present in the temple, where people experience many miracles.

That is the myth of Rakakshi.

I have known Goddess Rakakshi for many years, and while I had not originally intended to include her in this book, the inspiration to introduce her to you came from my Guru's recent trip to India in December 2024, when he visited the temple of this Goddess on the island of Rameshwaram, in Tamil Nadu.

I have visited this same temple every year between 2013 and 2020, attending ceremonies in Rakakshi's honor, and each time felt this place's powerful frequencies.

Also, soon after praying at this small but beautiful temple, I received miracles of healing or unexpected financial gifts—and so did my family, although they were not physically present.

I remember sitting at a ceremony next to a firepit, whose flames and pungent smoke rose high to the sky, making my eyes tear.

Several priests in white and red robes chanted mantras to the Goddess, as they put sacred woods, fragrant flowers, and abundant ghee into the fire. Their mantras echoed throughout the courtyard of the temple and beyond.

Even though I occasionally coughed due to the thick yet pleasant smoke, the ritual felt heavenly. We placed flower petals into the fire and chanted the special mantra containing powerful syllables.

The mantra of the Goddess also invoked the Chintamani gem and asked for blessings. With deep devotion to this generous female Angel—I would ask her for my heart's desire, and many times I received what I prayed for.

According to the Goddess tradition, those who ask with sincerity and faith will receive the fulfilment of their desires. This has also been my experience with Goddess Rakakshi Chintamani, and other higher beings.

It Is All in the Name

Rakakshi means "the One with a third eye full of fire." And the suffix "akshi" means Goddess, as in Goddess Meenakshi, Goddess Lakshmi, Goddess Kamakshi, and many others.

Dr. Pillai, an expert of Goddess worship, is a master who has been communicating with Rakakshi since a very young age, as he was born on this exotic and spiritual island named after a significant event mentioned in the epic Ramayana.

In fact, historical records in India reveal that 35,000 years ago, King Rama set out to defeat Ravana, an evil king who had kidnapped Sita, Rama's wife. Ravana was known as a demonic being for his extreme cruelty and reigned over Lanka—today's Sri Lanka. Also, the Ramayana mentioned a huge bridge linking Rameshwaram and Lanka at that time. Interestingly, "expert" historians, geologists, and academics have denied the existence of that bridge.

But today's satellite images confirm the presence of a now submerged bridge.

After killing Ravana and freeing Queen Sita, King Rama went to Rameshwaram to atone for his sin of taking a life. And the town was renamed Ram-Ishwara or the God of Rama—Shiva.

Also, Tamil Nadu, in Dr. Pillai's view, has a very ancient history—that began with Pleiadian ETs settling here a million years ago. It is also said that Tamil Nadu was the only region on Earth that was not submerged during the Great Flood, 11,000 years ago.

According to many experts of ET history, at a time when other evil races were tempering with our DNA to remove our supernormal powers, other benevolent races like those from the Pleiades star cluster respected Earth humans and protected them. But because benevolent cosmic beings do not interfere with humanity's free will, we need to ask for help—thus authorizing their intervention.

So, is it possible that Rakakshi with the flaming third eye came from the Pleiades? Was her flame an ET technology or fruit of her supernormal powers? No one really knows, although this Goddess is famous for her extraordinary gifts to both the local population and those who connect with her.

I was always eager to experience a vision of Rakakshi during my India trips to her temple—and have often seen glimpses of her pretty face and felt her energy.

Divine Intervention

During the trip of Dr. Pillai to Rameshwaram in November and December 2024, a great cyclone was building over this island off the coast of Tamil Nadu, the southernmost state of India. Dr. Pillai prayed to Rakakshi. "If you want me to visit you, please help. I leave the choice to you."

Soon after this prayer, the cyclone unexpectedly vanished, leaving everyone both surprised and ecstatic. So once again Dr. Pillai was able to visit this Goddess with whom he has been connecting since he was a child.

You, too, can pray to Rakakshi and ask her for anything you want—she is one of the most generous of all angelic beings—and always fulfills the devotees' requests.

I credit Rakakshi and other beloved Goddesses for supporting me in my spiritual work and success. One of the most recent miracles I have received is being featured in a life-changing movie, "Zero Limits," with Dr. Joe Vitale, the renowned author and star of the movie "The Secret."

Zero Limits is my ideal inspirational film, a documentary that proves how your dreams can and will come true and you can live a miraculous life. Every one of the successful people featured lives a zero-limits life with a grandiose mindset. In my part, I reveal what this unlimited mindset looks like when I work with my clients, and you can peek into a mini version of my zero-limits life.

In today's world filled with chaos, unpredictability, and fear, I'm so grateful that I can work at what I love the most—empowering others to live happier and more meaningful lives, while we both experience great spiritual growth.

I believe Zero Limits will show countless people how to acquire the skills of pure, unselfish love, forgiveness, and immense gratitude, which generate powerful fuel for miracles.

This movie—expected to premiere on June 26, 2025—and available on Amazon Prime in September 2025—will surely inspire and expand the horizons of many people and will encourage great transformation.

We are infinite beings who can do anything, and this movie fits perfectly into this new Golden Age of truth and mass awakening, when the Goddesses are pouring their love continuously onto the Earth plane—guiding us to joy, wealth, and fulfillment. And I strongly believe that "Zero Limits" brings you much-needed guidance with its many personal stories and real-life successes.

Try This

- Ask Rakakshi to bring you spiritual transformation and help you ascend to a higher dimension.
- Ask sincerely for something you really want, for example some jewelry, a home, or a job.
- Ask for the healing of an ailment.
- Ask her for happiness in your relationship and harmony with your beloved.
- Ask her for supernormal powers, such as enhanced intuition, higher wisdom, and the ability to manifest what you want.
- Ask for protection from evil forces.
- Thank Goddess Rakakshi with a smile.

EPILOGUE

HOW TO CONNECT WITH THE GODDESS

The Schumann Resonance explains the reason for spikes of common emotional and mental wavelengths among humans.

Moreover, the Schumann Resonance impacts our moods, reduces stress, and even lowers blood pressure. This is why group meditation can be very powerful and can positively influence our minds, the weather, and even lower the crime rates—as seen in a famous study known as the "Maharishi Experiment."

So, can we trust that meditation, prayer, and a belief in our own divinity can connect us with the Divine Feminine and bring us peace? I definitely believe so. The presence of the benevolent Sacred Feminine can also usher in a time of healing, miracle-making, and lasting prosperity all across the globe, as well as in our galaxy.

The Goddess in You

We have been collectively hypnotized to forget our past, along with names, dates, and beings associated with very important ancient events.

Now, we only have myths and legends capturing our hearts and speaking of the everlasting existence of the "seeders' and intergalactic beings who are in touch with our Source. They have now returned because our ascension and DNA upgrade have begun.

Myths are not metaphors, but rather eternal realities—and sometimes contain symbols that appear arcane at the level of our current consciousness.

But with a minimum of alertness, meditation and study, we will identify codes explaining our true history, and the story of our galaxy. According to scientist Gregg Braden, codes can also be found in our DNA. They speak of our intentional—not accidental—existence on Earth. This tells us that Gods or higher beings seeded life on Earth.

We are now collectively uncovering the hidden history of Earth, the truth about humanity and our encounters with many extraterrestrial races that visited us over millions of years. Many of these benevolent races are now back, and we will soon meet them.

Also, those who hunger for truth, revelations, and spiritual growth might need spiritual guidance and knowledge obtained from mystery schools. For this, I teach courses on spiritual awakening and activation of intuitive abilities. I also explain how our current cosmology does not tell our full history. And we have been unaware of the presence of star beings among us.

Fortunately, new science now confirms that the human genome finds no match among apes and hominids, and this should be startling even for hard-core skeptics. So not only are we not hominids, we are actually divine beings who originally came from the stars.

We are rising like human angels to a higher plane of existence.

But guess who has the power to kill all demons of ignorance, poverty and untruth? The Goddesses. With names such as Durga, Kali, Pratyangira, Varahi, and many more, at the end of a dark cycle—that we have just left—the Divine Goddess clears the slate.

The Divine Feminine brings in frequencies of love, empowerment for the righteous, punishment for the evil, and final victory to the good.

"Satyameva Jayate" or only truth triumphs—says a verse of the Atharva Veda, one of the four Vedas. The truth about our origins has returned and the Goddess, too. Everything will be revealed instantaneously, and you will know deep truths. And the Mother Goddess, who deeply loves you, will always be with you, inside of you.

May the light of the Goddess fulfill all your wishes and make you a beacon of the power of Shakti to create a blissful and magnificent life for you and others.

May you be free to express all your love and beauty and help others awaken to their own divinity and power.

Finally, devotional verses can build a bridge between the physical reality and the Divine Feminine. So, as I conclude, I send you much love, good wishes, and a short hymn I wrote in honor of the Goddess and your own divine nature.

> "As your soul turns to Her,
> Heaven opens vast golden doors,
> Luminescent flower petals fall at your feet.
> She has heard your call of despair,
> Now trillions of light beams from the galaxies
> Brighten your voyage through the ages.
> You are Her and She is You."

BIOGRAPHY

Lalitha Donatella Riback, International Bestselling Author, Transformational Mindset Coach, Entrepreneur, Spiritual Mentor.

She's a researcher of human consciousness, who has studied the Vedic culture of the yogis and sages of India for over 30 years. She holds a B.A. in Vedic arts and science.

Lalitha guides her students to their highest human potential, and has created ShreemLab, a coaching business that offers transformational courses for a miraculous life.

Her international bestselling books, studies with renowned mentors like Deepak Chopra and Dr. Baskaran Pillai, and an upcoming feature in Dr. Joe Vitale's movie, "Zero Limits," have established her as a respected authority in the field of spirituality for the new Golden Age.

Website: https://shreemlab.com

FUN FACTS

Lalitha was born on 1-11 at 11:11 am.

While living in India for 5 years, she traveled from the Himalayas to the southernmost point of Tamil Nadu, visiting nearly all the states, innumerable spiritual sites, and energetically powerful vortexes.

Lalitha lives in New York. When she's not writing, traveling, or meditating, she loves hiking, being in nature, and cooking healthy Ayurvedic foods with a touch of Italian cuisine.

BIBLIOGRAPHY

- A Place at the Altar: Priestesses in Republican Rome, by Meghan DiLuzio
- Secrets of the Siddhas, by Swami Muktananda
- The Sophia Code, by Kaia Ra
- Ayurvedic Healing, by Dr. David Frawley
- The Complete Book of Enoch, translation by R.H. Charles, W.R Morfill
- A Classic of Yoga and Tantra, by Siddhar Thirumoolar
- Prayers of the Cosmos, Translation by Dr. Neil Douglas-Klotz
- The Gospel of Mary Magdalene, translation by David Curtis
- The Gospel of Mary Magdalene, translation by Jeremy Payton
- The Gospel of Philip, The Nag Hammadi Library, translated by Wesley W. Isenberg
- Fractals of Reality: Living the Shri Chakra, by M.D. Kavitha Chinnaiyan
- The Golden Legend, by Archbishop Jacobus de Voragine
- Habits of a Godly Woman, by Joyce Meyer
- The Brides of Rome, by Debra May Macleod
- Everyday Bible, by Joyce Meyer
- Śrī Tripura Sundarī Devī Maha Vidya, by Dr. Ramamurthy Natarajan
- The Secret Life of Mother Mary, by Dr. Marguerite Mary Rigoglioso
- The Seeders, by Elena Danaan

Copyright © Lalitha Donatella Riback 2025

www.ingramcontent.com/pod-product-compliance
Lightning Source LLC
Chambersburg PA
CBHW060514090426
42735CB00011B/2219